DOUBLE ANOINTING

R.T. KENDALL

CHARISMA
HOUSE

Most Charisma Media products are available at special quantity discounts for bulk purchase for sales promotions, premiums, fund-raising, and educational needs. For details, call us at (407) 333-0600 or visit our website at www.charismamedia.com.

DOUBLE ANOINTING by R. T. Kendall
Published by Charisma House, an imprint of Charisma Media
600 Rinehart Road, Lake Mary, Florida 32746

Visit the author's website at www.rtkendallministries.com.

Cataloging-in-Publication Data is on file with the Library of Congress.

International Standard Book Number: 978-1-63641-124-8
E-book ISBN: 978-1-63641-125-5

22 23 24 25 26—9 8 7 6 5 4 3 2 1
Printed in the United States of America

To Colin and Amanda

CONTENTS

FOREWORD

ELIJAH. HE STANDS alone among the Old Testament prophets. Power over nature. Fire falling from Heaven in response to his intercession. Departing earth without physical death. Years later his appearance on the Mount of Transfiguration with Moses affirms his unique stature. Yet there was another who both asked for and received a double portion of Elijah's anointing, a man who performed twice the number of Elijah's miracles. This man was Elisha.

He is often an enigma. Like Elijah, he appeared from nowhere. Instructed by God to anoint him as his successor, Elijah found Elisha in obscurity, occupied in his plowing and labor. He did not come from one of the prophetic schools. He had no peers or prophetic heritage prior to his call. He left no disciple of note. Following years of service, Elisha prevailed upon his relationship with Elijah with an ambitious request: "Give me a double portion of your anointing." Who asks such a thing of a prophet like Elijah?

Remarkable in the ministry of Elisha are the miracles that reflected those of his mentor yet also foreshadowed those of Jesus. Elisha: the feeding of the hundred and the multiplication of bread (2 Kings 4:42–44). Jesus: the multiplication of the loaves and fishes (Matt. 14:13–21). Elisha: the miracle of the oil being multiplied (2 Kings 4:4–7). Jesus: the turning of water into wine at Cana (John 2:1–11).

Elisha: the resurrection of the Shunammite's son (2 Kings 4:18–36). Jesus: the resurrection of Lazarus (John 11).

From audiences with kings to meeting the practical needs of a widow, we find in Elisha a human, compassionate dimension that it seemed his mentor often lacked. Quite different from the life of Elijah, who neither experienced illness nor tasted death, Elisha suffered from a very human illness and died a very human death. Yet even after his death a residual anointing was found in his bones that would raise the dead.

There are numerous books about Elijah, including an excellent one by R. T. Kendall. Yet few works exist devoted to Elisha, and so this book is much needed. The illumination and insight that Dr. Kendall brings to both the man and ministry of Elisha are profound. This is much more than staid exegesis. The principles and application that he draws from the well of Elisha's life are critical to this hour of opportunity for the church.

I have long been fascinated with Elisha. I have also long admired Dr. Kendall. It is a great honor to put the words of this foreword alongside his. Thank you, Dr. Kendall, for this privilege, and thank you also for yet another great book, one that is essential to Spirit-empowered ministry in our age.

—JIM CRITCHER
SENIOR LEADERSHIP TEAM, GRACE COVENANT CHURCH
CHANTILLY, VIRGINIA

PREFACE

I FIRST PREACHED THROUGH the life of Elisha at London's Kensington Temple (KT). Pastor Colin Dye kindly asked us to spend six months a year in London, and it was during one of those six-month eras that I chose to speak on Elisha. I had preached on Elijah at Westminster Chapel, this being one of my last sermon series there. That series became a book called *These Are the Days of Elijah*. Having decided to make my next teaching series at The Cove in the summer of 2020, it made sense to turn these studies on Elisha into a book as well. Each of the chapters in this book should be treated as a standalone text that examines the scriptural story of Elisha chronologically, as we encounter it in the book of 2 Kings.

I want to thank Steve and Joy Strang of Charisma House for publishing this book. My thanks especially to Debbie Marrie, my editor, for being so easy and pleasant to work with. Most of all I thank my wife, Louise—my best friend and critic—for her wisdom and encouragement.

I thank Pastor Jim Critcher, part of the senior leadership team at Grace Covenant Church of Chantilly, Virginia, for writing the foreword to this book. He himself has been a student of 2 Kings generally and the life of Elisha especially and has been an encouragement to me.

I dedicate this book to our beloved friends, Colin and Amanda Dye, now in retirement after an incredible thirty-year ministry at Kensington Temple. Their legacy stands alongside the previous great men of God—historic stalwarts in Elim—who made KT a world-class church.

—R. T. Kendall
Nashville, Tennessee, September 2021

INTRODUCTION

ELISHA, ELIJAH'S SUCCESSOR, made the cheekiest, most audacious, and most ambitious request of any found in the entire Bible. He asked for a "double portion" of Elijah's anointing (2 Kings 2:9).

He had already received Elijah's mantle—and what a gift it was! But he was not content with that; he wanted more. Indeed he wanted *double* the anointing of Elijah.

And yet can you blame him? How do you suppose you would have felt had you personally witnessed this request? Would you have resented Elisha for this? Would you have been a bit irked that Elisha thought of this? On the other hand, "Ye have not, because ye ask not," according to James 4:2 (KJV). Bold and astonishing though this request may have been, what harm was there in asking? And what, lo and behold, if such a request was granted?

It was. Many of us would welcome such a gift—if offered. It would be hard to believe such was on offer, too good to be true! So don't resent Elisha for this request (if this thought crosses your mind), but rather admire him for his crude audacity. The first British missionary, William Carey (1761–1834), was known for saying this: "Expect great things from God, attempt great things for God."[1] God uses ambitious people. Martin Luther (1483–1546) is often quoted as saying, "God uses sex to drive a man to marriage, ambition to drive a man to service, fear to drive a man to faith."[2]

In any case, God granted Elisha's request.

The anointing is the power of the Holy Spirit that enables one's gift to function with ease. The anointing is what comes easy. If you go outside your anointing, you struggle. Stay within it, and you are at ease.

What Elisha asked for was a double portion of Elijah's "spirit." I take this to mean a double measure of the Holy Spirit given to Elijah, not meaning his natural gift. Elisha did not ask to be a clone of Elijah and have twice his talent or success. But one cannot be sure exactly what Elisha was asking for. According to Romans 12:3, each child of God has a measure of faith. This means a limit. No one has perfect faith—the faith of God that Jesus had (John 3:34). We are given a limit. Elijah had a limit, a measure of the Holy Spirit. You could say he had a very high level of the Spirit. Yes. And Elisha, Elijah's chosen successor, asked for twice the measure Elijah had!

If you are annoyed that someone would ask for twice the anointing of an Elijah, so too was Elijah himself. Elijah was not thrilled with this request. "You have asked a hard thing," he said (2 Kings 2:10). Was Elijah a bit jealous that Elisha might have double his success? Some think that Elijah did not have a fatherly spirit, that he resented Elisha's request. That said, Elijah agreed to Elisha's request on the condition that Elisha personally witness the actual, literal moment that Elijah was transferred to Heaven. Here is what Elijah said to Elisha:

> You have asked a hard thing; yet, if you see me as I am being taken from you, it shall be so for you, but if you do not see me, it shall not be so.
>
> —2 KINGS 2:10

The Bible says that as they went on and talked, behold, chariots of fire and horses of fire separated the two of them.

> And Elijah went up by a whirlwind into heaven. And Elisha saw it and he cried, 'My father, my father! The chariots of Israel and its horsemen!' And he saw him [Elijah] no more.
>
> —2 KINGS 2:11–12

What a glorious end to the life and ministry of Elijah. What a promising beginning to the ministry of Elisha.

It would seem that Elisha's double anointing was calculated in terms of quantity rather than quality. For example, Elijah had around seven miracles, depending on how you judge him and his situation. Elisha had perhaps fourteen miracles, thus confirming how he experienced a double measure of the Spirit. However, once Elisha died, he was largely forgotten. Elisha died a natural death (2 Kings 13:20). People still spoke of Elijah. Malachi prophesied that Elijah, who did not have a natural death, would appear later (Mal. 4:5–6). This was fulfilled in the ministry of John the Baptist (Luke 1:13–20). It was Elijah who appeared with Moses on the Mount of Transfiguration (Matt. 17:3).

These things said, some of Elisha's miracles were quite different from Elijah's. Indeed some of them were breathtakingly astounding. How wonderful it would be if God raised up an Elisha in our day! James speaks of how Elijah was just like us in his human nature (James 5:17). The same could be said of Elisha. There was nothing supernatural about him. He was very ordinary. Yet we are about to discover, through the life of the prophet Elisha, how God can take the ordinary and do something extraordinary.

CHAPTER 1

THE CALLING
OF ELISHA

So he departed from there and found Elisha the son
of Shaphat, who was plowing with twelve yoke of
oxen in front of him, and he was with the twelfth.
Elijah passed by him and cast his cloak upon him.
And he left the oxen and ran after Elijah and
said, "Let me kiss my father and my mother, and
then I will follow you." And he said to him, "Go
back again, for what have I done to you?" And he
returned from following him and took the yoke
of oxen and sacrificed them and boiled their flesh
with the yokes of the oxen and gave it to the people,
and they ate. Then he arose and went after Elijah
and assisted him.

—1 KINGS 19:19–21

Only one life, t'will soon be past, only what's done
for Christ will last.

—C. T. STUDD (1860–1931)

ONE OF THE mysteries of both the Old Testament
and church history is why some great leaders
had successors and others did not. For example,
God chose Moses' successor but chose no successor to

Joshua. After Joshua died everyone did what was right "in their own eyes" (Judg. 21:25). It seems reasonable to assume that a successor to Joshua could have led Israel to avoid that unspeakably bad era.

Likewise, God raised up Elijah. He came in from out of the blue. God chose Elijah's successor—Elisha—but there was no successor to Elisha.

Elisha was God's idea. For reasons one cannot understand, God was thinking of Israel's immediate future when he told Elijah to give his mantle to Elisha. But why not a successor to Elisha?

Most unusual leaders are not succeeded by great men. There was no successor to Paul. Or to Augustine. Or Luther. Or Jonathan Edwards.

The question therefore may be asked: Why did God grant a successor to Moses in the first place? Or to Elijah?

We have no idea how Elijah was called, but we know how Elisha was called. It was God's idea from the beginning.

When we use the word *call* or *calling* to refer to one's ministry, specialty, or career, it is good to remember that someone initiated such a call. Moses did not call himself. Elisha did not call himself. Jeremiah did not appoint himself but says that God "appointed" him to be a "prophet to the nations" (Jer. 1:5).

Likewise, when Paul refers to the "called" in Romans 1:6 and Romans 8:30, God is the initial "cause." Although Paul became aware of his being called on the road to Damascus (Acts 22:6–16), he said he was actually called before he was born (Gal. 1:15).

So with all of us. We cannot answer a call until we have been consciously called. If we take a few moments to contemplate this kind of thinking, we will almost certainly come to the same conclusion Charles Spurgeon (1834–1892) came to. He saw that God was "at the bottom of it all." We can take no credit for this. It is because God first loved us (1 John 4:19) that Jesus chose us (John 15:16).

Elisha could take no credit that he was called to be Elijah's successor. He did nothing to deserve it. He was in the field with oxen. God found him. What were Elisha's qualifications? You tell me! What are your qualifications? What are mine? God sees in all of us what people do not see. People look on the outward appearance, but God looks at the heart (1 Sam. 16:7). Spurgeon was rejected by Regent's Park College! G. Campbell Morgan (1863–1945) was rejected by the Methodist church because he did not have the makings of a preacher!

It did not take long for Elisha to develop an ambition to want double Elijah's anointing. He had not been in the battle that long. Perhaps it was ambition in Elisha that God saw?

What is fascinating is that Elisha showed a dogged ambition to get Elijah's anointing before he was given a choice about it. Knowing somehow that Elijah would be taken away at any moment, Elisha stayed in Elijah's face sixty seconds a minute all day long. It was as if he had already been told that he must literally *see* Elijah's ascension to Heaven. For example, Elijah began saying to Elisha, "Please stay here," pretending to go to Bethel, Jericho, or Jordan. But Elisha responded in a second, "As the LORD lives, and as you yourself live, I will not leave you" (2 Kings 2:2–6).

When God calls a person to ministry, either He has pre-gifted such a person or, in any case, ensures that such a man or woman has the appropriate talent to do what He has in mind for them. Spurgeon said that if God calls a man to preach he will give that man a pair of lungs. It was more than a willing heart that George Beverly Shea (1909–2013) needed to be Billy Graham's (1918–2018) beloved Gospel singer. He had a voice that comes perhaps once in a generation.

But whatever was it in Elisha? Only God knew. Moreover, God knew that Elisha would stay next to Elijah nonstop all day long in order not to miss the challenge of his life.

Would you like to have a double anointing? What if it depended on how hard you tried to get it? Frankly, if I personally thought that it depended on me and my earnestness, I would mimic Elisha! Yes, I would do what he did. I would pray more, read my Bible more, study more, get to know more, get people to lay their hands on me who had any bit of power—or whatever I thought it would take. Because I identify with Elisha.

We only have one life to live for Christ. Only what is done for Him will last, said C. T. Studd. I would rather face the Lord at the judgment seat of Christ knowing I did all I could possibly think of than wait for the sovereignty of God (which I believe in with all my heart) to make things happen.

I don't have a prophetic gift that I know of. I wish I did. I am a Bible teacher. That's it. But because Paul said we should covet earnestly the best gifts, I will tell you now that I pray daily (and have done for a good while) for the gifts of wisdom, prophecy, discerning of spirits, miracles, and healing. On top of that I ask all the time—daily, to be transparently honest—for double the anointing I now have. I don't understand the Bible nearly as well as I want to. Whether God will grant this, even in part, in my lifetime, only He knows. And since both gifts and calling are without repentance (that means no amount of godliness or zeal can bring on these gifts—Romans 11:29), all I can do is ask.

Would you like a double anointing? What would that be like in your life? What if it were double what you have now? What if it were double of what another person has? Elisha wanted double what Elijah had. After all, there had never been a prophet like Elijah.

Anointing, such as we see in 1 John 2:20-27, comes from the Greek *chrio*: to smear as with an ointment[1]; we get *Christ* from the root word. Christ means Anointed One, Messiah.

As I said, Jesus had the Spirit without measure or limit (John 3:34). You and I have a measure of the Spirit, a measure of faith (Rom. 12:3). Jesus had all of the Holy Spirit that there is. You and I have a little bit of the Holy Spirit. Even if we are "filled" with the Spirit, we are filled with a little bit of the Holy Spirit. Jesus was filled with the Spirit and had all there is of the Holy Spirit.

How do you discover your anointing? Anointing can also be one's gifting. You begin at the natural level: What are you already good at? What comes easy? Chances are your anointing by the Spirit will be an extension of what you are by common grace (God's special grace in nature). The hardest and most humbling thing to do is to discover the limits of your anointing.

Nobody can do everything. Be honest: What is it you simply are unable to do—and what are you good at? For example, are you a computer genius, brilliant in physics,

5

good at public speaking, skilled at nursing? God never promotes us to the level of our incompetence. Laurence J. Peter (1919–1990) wrote *The Peter Principle*, the idea being that everyone is promoted to the level of their incompetence. This is often true, but God never promotes us to the level of our incompetence.

There are three references I know of that refer to what I would call a double anointing:

> Instead of your shame there shall be a double portion; instead of dishonor they shall rejoice in their lot; therefore in their land they shall possess a double portion; they shall have everlasting joy.
>
> —ISAIAH 61:7

> Return to your stronghold, O prisoners of hope; today I declare that I will restore to you double.
>
> —ZECHARIAH 9:12

> Please let there be a double portion of your spirit on me.
>
> —2 KINGS 2:9

And yet I am not sure what double anointing means! It is hard to imagine a greater miracle than the fire that came down at Mount Carmel. Elisha saw nothing of this.

I have asked for a double anointing for years—that is, double what I now have. I have assumed this to refer to quality, that is, to grasp the meaning of certain biblical verses I do not understand. I could write a book titled *Verses in the Bible I Don't Understand.*

I would love to have the gift of healing. I have seen a few people healed in my ministry, but not a lot. I would enjoy having a "word" for people—call it prophetic or a word of knowledge. My gifting, it seems to me, is teaching the Bible. A double anointing in my case, I think, would mean that *I would find understanding the Bible twice as easy, twice as quick—that I would have double the ability to see the hidden meaning of Scripture.*

What do you suppose a double anointing means in your case? Be true to yourself; come to terms with your natural gift—what already comes easy for you. For example, is it understanding electronics, medicine, law, politics, or poetry?

Your gift could be insignificant (as far as you are concerned), but consider Joseph's gift of having dreams and interpreting them. There is something you can do that nobody else can do as well.

> What no eye has seen, nor ear heard, nor the heart
> of man imagined, what God has prepared for those
> who love him.
> —1 Corinthians 2:9 (See also Isaiah 64:4)

These verses provide a vague encouragement to have more of God than one has at the moment. Paul invited us to explore unlimited possibilities when he said for us to desire earnestly the "higher" gifts (1 Cor. 12:31).

Why not a double anointing? Chances are most of us would love double of what we now have. But hopefully with this condition we would thereby glorify God twice as much! This would not be to enhance our ego. It would be solely for the honor and glory of God. If not, *away with such foolish ambition*!

Elisha was an anticipated man. That means we are not

surprised to see him emerge later. Unlike Elijah, who showed up out of the blue with no background or credentials that we know of, Elisha is found by Elijah.

We may assume Elisha would be Elijah's successor. As I observed, sometimes God gives a great person a successor: Joshua was a successor to Moses. Solomon was a worthy successor to King David.

Elisha was an average man. He was common, ordinary. As Elijah was just like us "with a nature like ours" (James 5:17), so too Elisha. It is so encouraging to know that the Elijahs and Elishas of this world are chosen from common, ordinary stock.

Not so Moses; of the tribe of Levi, he was unusual from birth (Exod. 2:2)—a fine child, fair. So too Saul of Tarsus was groomed for greatness. He had a very high IQ and the very best education, sitting at the feet of Gamaliel the Jewish scholar (Acts 22:3).

Our man Elisha was ordinary, typical, average. He asked Elijah permission to say goodbye to his parents. Nothing spectacular about Elisha. Does that encourage you? It encourages me.

Most believers are chosen from what is "average":

> For consider your calling, brothers: not many of you were wise according to worldly standards, not many were powerful, not many were of noble birth. But God chose what is foolish in the world to shame the wise; God chose what is weak in the world to shame the strong; God chose what is low and despised in the world, even things that are not, to

bring to nothing things that are, so that no human
being might boast in the presence of God.
—1 Corinthians 1:26-29

God determined that the Christian faith would bring
Him glory because it could never be said that the more
intelligent chose Jesus. Some may wish it were like that!
But the Einsteins of this world miss the greatest glory
imaginable. Why are some saved and others not? There
is no rhyme or reason save this: the sovereign work of the
Spirit (John 6:44).

Lady Selina Hastings, Countess of Huntingdon (1707–
1791), the benefactor of George Whitefield (1714–1770),
rejoiced that she was saved by the letter "M." This is
because Paul said that not *many* were of noble birth. He
did not say not *any*!

The Christian faith is so designed that God gets all the
glory. It is not offered to the rich or famous, nor to those
who have talent or will make the church look good. It is
offered to ordinary people—like you and me.

There have been exceptions in history. Sometimes God
saves a St. Augustine (AD 354–430), a Thomas Aquinas
(1225–1274), a St. Anselm (1033–1109), a Martin Luther, a
John Calvin (1509–1564), a Jonathan Edwards (1703–1758).
When people like these are converted, the world is deeply
influenced. Why not more? You tell me! Probably so no
one can say that Christianity is for the most intelligent.

In any case, both Elijah and Elisha were ordinary people.

Elisha was, as we saw, an ambitious man. He turned
out to be extremely ambitious; not sure where that came
from unless God was behind it. Ambition is connected to

one's motivation, drive, and desire to succeed. Like it or not, it is ambitious people who get things done.

Moses was ambitious. Why ever would he leave the palace of Pharaoh for the sake of the "reproach of Christ"? The answer is simple: he was looking ahead to his "reward" (Heb. 11:24–26). He was no fool! Caleb was an ambitious man; at age eighty-five he aspired to more than what he had ("Give me this mountain"—Joshua 14:12, KJV).

I was an ambitious vacuum cleaner salesman in our early marriage. I would leave the office early and start knocking on doors and return before noon with a sale while the other salesmen were still drinking coffee. One sense of ambition is by common grace, what God gives by creation (which is quite apart from saving grace).

Thank God for your ambition. Channel that ambition into wanting the full honor and glory of God. Paul in his old age had this ambition to know Christ (Phil. 3:8–9). We should all have this ambition. Ask God to give you a double anointing to want a greater knowledge of Christ.

Elisha was an ambitious man. But there was more. He was an answered man. He asked. God answered Elisha's prayer. James said that we have not because we ask not (Jas. 4:2).

> Ask of me and I will make the nations your heritage.
> —Psalm 2:8

> Ask, and it will be given you; seek, and you will find; knock, and it will be opened to you. For everyone who asks receives, and the one who seeks finds, and to the one who knocks it will be opened.
> —Matthew 7:7–8

I sought the LORD, and he answered me.
                              —PSALM 34:4, NIV

What have you asked of the Lord?

As for ambition, do not forget that you could gain the whole world and lose your soul (Mark 8:36). So don't be a fool! Be *ambitious for your own soul.*

> Only one life, t'will soon be past,
> Only what's done for Christ will last.

CHAPTER 2

WHEN GOD
SHOWS UP

Then he took hold of his own clothes and tore them in two pieces. And he took up the cloak of Elijah that had fallen from him and went back and stood on the bank of the Jordan. Then he took the cloak of Elijah that had fallen from him and struck the water, saying, "Where is the LORD, the God of Elijah?" And when he had struck the water, the water was parted to the one side and to the other, and Elisha went over.

—2 KINGS 2:12–14

Though you have not seen him, you love him. Though you do not now see him, you believe in him and rejoice with joy that is inexpressible and filled with glory, obtaining the outcome of your faith, the salvation of your souls.

—1 PETER 1:8–9

Faith is the refusal to panic.

—DR. MARTYN LLOYD-JONES (1899–1981)

I HAVE HAD A theory about 1 Peter 1:9 for over sixty years: that it contains a double meaning. Peter talks about the "end of your faith, even the salvation of your souls" (KJV). The Greek word for *end* comes from *telos*—meaning "end," "goal," or "outcome."[1] But my theory is that *telos* can mean literally *the end*. Could Peter be encouraging one to trust God, to believe, to hold on until faith becomes sight? For example, when "every eye shall see him"—Jesus—at the second coming (Rev. 1:7), no one will need faith. The second coming will be the end of faith, for sure. I therefore posit my theory that Peter is encouraging one not only to persevere until we get to Heaven but even now to expect God to show up powerfully, unmistakably, miraculously, and with no doubt whatever. As I will make clear, this would not be a permanent experience; it is a temporary joy when the need for faith seems redundant. But the need for faith will indeed return, I assure you.

My theory was born on October 31, 1955, when I was driving in my car on old US Route 41 on my way from Palmer to Nashville, Tennessee. That is when God showed up with such glory, power, and reality that the person of Jesus was more real to me than the Tennessee countryside around me. For the next several days I was drawn to 1 Peter 1:9 for some reason. I have shared my theory of 1 Peter 1:9 with no one, only wishing that my old friend Dr. Michael Eaton were still alive, he possibly being the only person who would understand this and not reject me as a heretic!

Be that as it may, I only know that Elisha was needing to see God personally for himself moments after Elijah was taken to Heaven. So he asked, "Where is the LORD, the God of Elijah?" (2 Kings 2:14).

Have you ever needed God to show up? Have you ever had a desire, a deep need, to see for yourself whether the God of the Bible is real?

That is what Elisha was feeling.

If I may go back to my experience of October 31, 1955—when I was baptized with the Holy Spirit—I had the exact need of Elisha that morning. I had been in agony of spirit. I was crying out, "Lord, where are You? What is going on? Am I not saved?"

A second later I saw with my own eye—spiritual eye, mind you—the person of Jesus Christ interceding for me at the right hand of God. I burst into tears and from that moment became a spectator. I watched from then on.

I suspect Elisha was feeling lonely after Elijah was transported to glory. He needed to know whether he would see the glory of the Lord for himself. So he asked: "Where is the Lord, the God of Elijah?"

Whether Elisha was a bit nervous, I don't know. Whether he began to doubt, I don't know. I do know for sure that Elisha needed to know *now* that God had not deserted him. It is not unlike when Moses was told, "Lift up your staff, and stretch out your hand over the sea and divide it, that the people of Israel may go through the sea on dry ground" (Exod. 14:16). *And it happened.*

There comes that moment in every Christian life when one so earnestly wants to know whether God is real or not. We need to see Him work! Not that any one of us ever outgrows the need for faith. No. I am not saying that. But we nevertheless need to have that moment, however brief, when God witnesses to us with such depth and joy and ecstasy that we are left speechless.

That is what Elisha needed. And that is what he got.

The double portion of Elijah's spirit was now confirmed in earnest. Elisha did not need twice the level of Elijah's power to see the Jordan River part. But he was now assured that Elijah's mantle had fallen on him. Not merely the physical cloak but what that cloak symbolized, namely, power.

The parting of the Jordan was the first installment of Elisha's power. Elisha walked across the river bottom to the other side.

Would you like a double anointing of the Holy Spirit? What is required to get this? Is it within reach of ordinary people like you and me? When Elisha asked Elijah for a double portion of his spirit, we know what Elijah replied as a condition: Elisha must be *looking at Elijah at the moment* he was taken up (2 Kings 2:10). It was black and white; if Elisha had his head turned and Elijah was taken up at that moment, too bad for Elisha—there would be no second chance.

A company of some fifty prophets had begun to say to Elisha that the Lord would take Elijah away that day. Who were these prophets? Where had they come from? It is hard to tell. These were proof that Elijah was not the only prophet around at that time.

But why would not God raise up one of these to succeed Elijah? Sometimes God seeks His servants from a group already trained and prepared; sometimes He picks someone who does not appear to be qualified—so with Elijah finding Elisha. My predecessor, Dr. Martyn Lloyd-Jones, had no theological training. But he was the greatest teacher I ever had.

What exactly Elijah required of Elisha to get this double portion Elisha somehow knew already; this is why

Elisha would not leave him for one second on that day. Elisha used "oath language" to Elijah. He swore by the living God he would not leave Elijah's side (2 Kings 2:2, 4, 6). This is the language Elijah used when he first confronted Ahab (1 Kings 17:1), but then it was a prophecy. Here it is not a prophecy but a promise—with an oath—that under no circumstances would Elisha leave Elijah.

Have you ever made a vow? According to the Old Testament, it is better not to make a vow than to make it and not fulfill it (Eccles. 5:4–5).

One might think God would choose one of those prophets who were engaging in these conversations. God is not bound by tradition or our natural expectancy. He frequently chooses to work where no one would have thought, or He chooses people we would not have suspected. It would not be surprising that any one of these prophets secretly hoped to get Elijah's mantle.

A whirlwind is a tornado, when a violent wind comes swooping down and takes things elsewhere. A whirlwind took Elijah away.

The prophets thought (wrongly) that Elijah was taken and carried off not far away, but Elisha (rightly) told them not to bother to look for him.

Where did he go? To Heaven: Moses and Elijah appeared with Jesus at the Transfiguration hundreds of years later (Matt. 17:1–8). Not one of those prophets got it right when it came to figuring out where Elijah had been taken. It is a reminder that having a prophetic gift does not give you unlimited access to God. The problem is that some people with a prophetic gift may fancy they are the Elijahs or Elishas of this world. This is possibly why they don't want to admit to getting it wrong when it comes to presidential elections. They apparently want people to respect them and look up to them. This may be precisely why such people are *not* granted this "inside knowledge." Perhaps it is why God chose Elisha and not one of those fifty prophets.

What was Elisha thinking when he asked for a double portion of Elijah's spirit? Was he thinking of double the power or quality of miracles? Was he thinking of having twice as many miracles (which seems to be the way the prayer was answered)? Was he thinking of the honor of God—or his own honor? And ego? And reputation?

A friend of mine said, "What faith Elisha had to ask for that!" I reply: Was it great faith or a big ego?

We know that Elijah himself had a huge ego. Elisha's bold request suggests he already had an ego equivalent to Elijah's. Many of us have an unrealistic view of many of God's servants.

THEY ALL HAVE BIG EGOS

I once thought that true men of God were so humble and meek and so like Jesus that they were borderline angelic. I once regarded the evangelist Glyn Grosse (not his real name) as the godliest man I ever laid eyes on. He was known widely as a man of prayer. I drove from Palmer to Chattanooga, Tennessee, to have him pray for me and lay his hands on me. I will never forget that day as long as I live. As he prayed, I felt so honored and assured that I would somehow emerge with more power—that is, until he followed his prayer immediately with these very words: "Don't tell anyone my age."

I was stunned. I said to myself, "The only thing Brother

Grosse thought of as he prayed for me was that he had revealed his age to me earlier." It was all I could think about from that moment—perhaps my first firsthand proof that the best of men are men at best. Indeed we are all frail, fragile, and fleshly servants of God. I have lived long enough to report that every person I have ever admired too much sooner or later disappointed me. It is not their fault; I needed to learn the lesson about human depravity and weakness. This is why James says what he does about Elijah (Jas. 5:17). I would not want you to know what I know about myself! I am sure that would be true also about Elijah or the apostle Paul. John Stott, one of the saintliest men I have ever known, said to me when I saw him for the last time: "If you really knew me you would spit in my face."

There was a consensus among these fifty prophets that Elijah would be taken from them that day. How did they know? Prophetic unity is a good thing. I have got to know quite a number of prophetic people. I'm sorry, but there is a rivalry among most of them. These fifty prophets for some reason wanted Elisha to know they had this insight that Elijah would be taken away that day. Elisha replied that he too knew but did not want to talk about it (2 Kings 2:3, 5.) Why did he not want to talk about it? Was he too emotionally involved? Perhaps the thought of losing Elijah was too painful for him.

You could say that the fifty prophets had a cooperative anointing. They agreed together that Elijah would be taken. In this there was no rivalry or dissenting opinion. There was unity of opinion and purpose. The disciples were of one accord on the day of Pentecost: "all together in one place" (Acts 2:1). The disciples were of one accord when facing persecution and praying together (Acts 4:24). They lifted up their voices together; they prayed aloud. Luke is sharing the unity of theology and purpose represented by their prayer. Yes, they each prayed aloud. Luke conveyed the thrust, the theology, and the theme of their praying.

As I said, Elisha surmised all day long that such a condition—keep your eyes fastened on Elijah—was somehow relevant. He would not take his eyes off Elijah even before this condition was made explicit. This reminds me of the psalmist's prayers:

> Behold, as the eyes of servants look to the hand of their master, as the eyes of a maidservant to the hand of her mistress, so our eyes look to the LORD our God till he has mercy on us.
> —PSALM 123:2

> But I wait for the LORD, my soul waits, and in his word I hope; my soul waits for the LORD more than watchmen for the morning, more than watchmen for the morning.
> —PSALM 130:5-6

Sometimes God plays hard to get. Jesus, on the road to Emmaus, appeared to keep going when the two men begged him to stay (Luke 24:28). It is what Jesus wanted from them.

Jesus, walking on water, appeared to pass by the disciples (Mark 6:48), but He wanted them to reach out to Him.

Elisha met the condition that Elijah stipulated: Elisha was staring at Elijah when the whirlwind came.

Elisha tore his clothes (2 Kings 2:12). Why? Tearing

one's clothes was a dramatic gesture to express the emotion of grief (Gen. 37:34; Judg. 11:34–35; 2 Sam. 13:30–31; Job 2:12; Mark 14:63). Was he in grief because Elijah was taken? He must have been overjoyed that he saw Elijah leave!

I don't know why Elisha tore his clothes. To be sure, it was an emotional moment. With Elijah gone, Elisha was now on his own for the first time. He knew he saw Elijah go to Heaven. He knew he had Elijah's mantle, or cloak.

As Dr. Lloyd-Jones once put it, "Faith is a refusal to panic."[2]

Elisha asks, "Where now is the LORD, the God of Elijah?" He takes the mantle of Elijah—the entry point into the supernatural—and dips it into the water of the Jordan River. Before his very own eyes, the water divides to the right and to the left.

It was happening: Elijah's anointing now obviously continued on Elisha. He may have thought, "I can't believe I am doing this." But he would always know; it wasn't Elisha doing this; he could take no credit for the anointing. What Elisha would experience in the coming years defied a natural explanation.

I once asked the late Carl F. H. Henry (1913–2003): "If you had your life to live over, what would you do differently?" His eyes moistened. Then he answered: "I would try to remember that only God can turn the water into wine."

When you see the anointing in your own life, at work, at your job, with people—you know it is not you. Never, ever will you be able to take credit for any level of anointing. It is all down to the *God* of Elijah.

Perhaps you will know this old spiritual:

> Swing low, sweet chariot. Coming for to carry me
>   home...
> I looked over Jordan, and what did I see...a band
>   of angels coming after me...
> If you get there before I do...tell all my friends I'm
>   coming too.

There are at last two sources for this old spiritual. First, the account of Elijah being taken up in a chariot of fire. A chariot was a two-wheeled vehicle drawn by horses—used in war in ancient times. What was the fire? Possibly the same kind of fire that Moses saw at the burning bush and at Sinai. It was possibly the same kind of fire that fell on Mount Carmel. What a welcome home! What an honor and affirmation of Elijah. This was the same Elijah who falsely claimed, "I alone am left" (1 Kings 18:22, NKJV). It was the same Elijah who ran from Jezebel—what a weak man he was without the anointing. He was now given a welcome greater than any national leader. Greater than holding up a gold medal at the Olympics.

Second, the angelic escort given to Lazarus in the parable of the rich man and Lazarus: one went to Heaven, namely, the poor man, Lazarus. The black slaves in the Deep South of Alabama would have identified with Lazarus. The rich man (we don't know his name) went to Hell. Jesus said, "Rejoice that your names are written in heaven" (Luke 10:20).

"Where is the LORD, the God of Elijah?," then, is the question Elisha asked when he came to the river Jordan. He had seen Elijah being taken up in the whirlwind; Elisha knew that he met the condition.

When he dipped Elijah's cloak into the Jordan, the

water parted. Faith was required for him to dip the cloak into the water. But when the water began to part, faith ended. For a while.

Have you met the condition? If so, the water will part for you too.

God showed up. Exactly when Elisha needed to see God work.

CHAPTER 3

WHEN GOD SEEMS TO MAKE NO SENSE

Now the men of the city said to Elisha, "Behold, the situation of this city is pleasant, as my lord sees, but the water is bad, and the land is unfruitful." He said, "Bring me a new bowl, and put salt in it." So they brought it to him. Then he went to the spring of water and threw salt in it and said, "Thus says the LORD, 'I have healed this water; from now on neither death nor miscarriage shall come from it.'" So the water has been healed to this day, according to the word that Elisha spoke.

—2 KINGS 2:19–22

We serve this God not because He dances to our tune, but because we trust His preeminence in our lives.

—DR. JAMES DOBSON (1936–)

THERE ARE TIMES when it seems that God does not make sense, and I will show two examples in this chapter. The first is when Elisha makes a strange request regarding how to deal with bad water. The second is when God affirms Elisha's cursing of little boys for making fun of him.

> He went up from there to Bethel, and while he was going up on the way, some small boys came out of the city and jeered at him, saying, "Go up, you baldhead! Go up, you baldhead!" And he turned around, and when he saw them, he cursed them in the name of the Lord. And two she-bears came out of the woods and tore forty-two of the boys. From there he went on to Mount Carmel, and from there he returned to Samaria.
>
> —2 Kings 2:23–25

It did not take long for Elisha to get a reputation for being a prophet: "The spirit of Elijah is resting on Elisha" (2 Kings 2:15). Nor did it take a lot of discernment to figure this out. They saw firsthand the water of the Jordan parting before their very eyes. As soon as Elisha walked over to them on the bottom of the Jordan, they came to him and bowed to the ground before him (2 Kings 2:15). They no doubt had hoped that they too might have this anointing. They wanted unselfishly therefore to affirm not only Elisha but God Himself, who passed by them and put His hand on Elisha. It shows a unity that has not always characterized the people of God.

Gabriel's promise to Zechariah regarding John the Baptist was that the child would grow up and go before the Lord "in the spirit and power of Elijah" (Luke 1:17). The spirit of Elijah, however, was on Elisha centuries before it was on John the Baptist. Elisha's life would never be the same again.

Do you wish you had a prophetic gift? Caution: woe to you if you are given the undoubted gift of prophecy; people will look for you to give a word. I don't know if

Elisha was plagued with people always wanting a word, but nowadays that is the way it is. If I had a genuine prophetic gift, I think I would keep quiet about it as long as I could!

The "men of the city"—probably Jericho—came looking for Elisha. To whom much is given will much be required (Luke 12:48). Are you sure you want any of the more spectacular gifts of the Spirit? These prophets who affirmed Elisha obviously did not have great gifts. They should have known that Elijah could not be found.

Elisha now had an authority unlike anybody else; the men of the city now treated him as they would Elijah. They put a very difficult case to Elisha: "Behold, the situation of this city is pleasant, as my lord sees, but the water is bad, and the land is unfruitful" (2 Kings 2:19).

It is reasonable to assume if there is a person with the stature of Elijah or Elisha around, you expect such a prophet to speak to any situation—not just to one's personal issues. I am a bit sickened that there are people today who get hailed for being able to call out a name and address and birthdate of a person on the seventeenth row of a stadium of fifty thousand and not be warned of a pandemic that changes the world. Therefore, that Elisha would be asked to speak to a situation in Jericho that affects the entire area is what one would expect a true prophet to address: "the water is bad, and the land is unfruitful."

Elisha's rather strange solution: "Bring me a new bowl, and put salt in it" (2 Kings 2:20). No one questioned Elisha. They did what he requested. They brought it to him. He then went to the spring of water and threw salt in it and said: "Thus says the LORD, I have healed this water; from now on neither death nor miscarriage shall come from it" (v. 21). So the water has been healed "to this day, according to the word that Elisha spoke" (v. 22).

I have been to this very spring in Jericho. The water is sweet and good to drink even to this day.

We may ask two questions: (1) why "new" bowl and (2) why "salt"? This explains the title I have chosen for this chapter: "When God Seems to Make No Sense." This is a predictable pattern of God's ways over the centuries. God is like that; it is part of His "ways." God lamented that the people of Israel "have not known my ways" (Heb. 3:10).

So why is this word important: when God seems to make no sense? Whether it be God's strange request to Abraham to sacrifice Isaac (Gen. 22:2) or what was happening outside the city of Jerusalem on Good Friday, God loves to surprise the world by His wisdom. Indeed in this story are found the first rudiments of the Gospel. If you are not a Christian, this chapter can help you know how to become a Christian. Second, in this story of Elisha we should learn a lesson: don't try to figure God out; trust Him to know what He is up to.

"This town is well situated," the men of the city said to Elisha. "Location, location, location," as they say in real estate. Jericho is a lovely place, said to be the oldest city in the world. But the water was bad in those days and the land unproductive. Location means nothing if you can't eat or drink.

"Bring me a new bowl," Elisha requested. Why new? Couldn't they find an old bowl that would do just as well? Answer: God was going to do something new and different. God loves to do what is unprecedented. Not one person of faith in Hebrews 11 had the luxury of repeating what preceded them. Each one had to do what had never been done before. Here are two relevant passages:

> For my thoughts are not your thoughts, neither are your ways my ways, declares the LORD. For as the heavens are higher than the earth, so are my ways higher than your ways and my thoughts than your thoughts.
>
> —ISAIAH 55:8–9

> God chose what is foolish in the world to shame the wise; God chose what is weak in the world to shame the strong; God chose what is low and despised in the world, even things that are not, to bring to nothing things that are, so that no human being might boast in the presence of God.
>
> —1 CORINTHIANS 1:27–29

"Put salt in it," ordered Elisha. There was plenty of salt around. The Dead Sea, sometimes called the Salt Sea, is within walking distance of Jericho, and the Jordan River empties into it. As I said, sometimes God requires things of us that make no sense at the time.

Whatever can a new bowl and salt do to heal the land? The men of the city might have said, "Who does this Elisha think he is? We will not be treated as if we are stupid."

Whenever a reliable prophet puts a request that makes no sense, we should obey.

When we are desperate, we should obey. It was a simple request—nothing complicated about it. It made no sense. But the words were clear.

So too with the Gospel: it makes no sense, but the message is clear: the blood of Jesus will wash away your sin. Yes, it makes no sense, but the words are clear.

"So they brought it to him" (2 Kings 2:20). It was easy for them to do; they did not argue. We do the little things; God does the big things. Your task: look to Jesus.

> There is life for a look at the crucified one,
> There is life at this moment for thee;
> Then look, sinner, look unto him and be saved,
> Unto him who was nailed to the tree.
> —Amelia M. Hull (1812–1884)[1]

Jesus said, "For this is the will of my Father, that everyone who *looks on the Son* and believes in him should have eternal life, and I will raise him up on the last day" (John 6:40, emphasis added). As Charles Spurgeon put it, "Run to the cross. If you can't run, walk. If you can't walk, crawl. If you can't crawl, look." It is not great faith that saves; it is faith in a great Savior.

> Come, ye sinners, poor and needy,
> weak and wounded, sick and sore;
> Jesus ready stands to save you,
> full of pity, love and power.
>
> Come, ye thirsty, come and welcome,
> God's free bounty glorify;
> true belief and true repentance,
> ev'ry grace that brings you nigh.
>
> Let not conscience make you linger,
> nor of fitness fondly dream;
> all the fitness he requireth
> is to feel your need of Him.

Come, ye weary, heavy laden,
lost and ruined by the fall;
if you tarry till you're better,
you will never come at all.

—JOSEPH HART (1712–1768)[2]

How can supernatural restoration—the healing of bad water—happen by emptying a bowl of salt into bad water to make it sweet? What is the explanation? It is a mysterious explanation. Don't try to figure it out. Moses wanted to figure out how a bush could be on fire and not be consumed. God told him to take off his shoes and worship. It is a miraculous explanation. It begins with the Word of God: "This is what the Lord says" (v. 21). God is at the bottom of it all: "I have healed this water" (v. 21). Elisha gave a pronouncement: "Never again will it cause death or make the land unproductive" (v. 21, KJV). As I said, I have tasted this water. The spring exists in Jericho today.

At bottom, then, it is what *God* did. It is not what Elisha did; he was only the instrument. If God can heal water, He can heal you.

A Muslim lady in London was awakened in the night, hearing the word "Kendall." She wondered what it could mean. She decided the next morning to walk across the street to a Catholic church and light a candle. The dream was repeated several days later, with her still hearing "Kendall." She went to the Catholic church and lit another candle. But she said to a friend, "How can I learn about the Bible? Can I take a course online?" Her friend said, "Perhaps you should go to Westminster Chapel and listen to Dr. Kendall." At once she said, "Kendall. That is the word I heard." She went to Buckingham Chapel the following Friday evening. She said to Louise and me, "When I walked into the church, I knew I had come home." She was later miraculously healed of throat cancer. She was baptized and became a member of Westminster Chapel.

A man from Glasgow, Scotland, came to Westminster Chapel one Sunday morning. After communion we offered the anointing of oil to anyone who wanted healing. He said to himself, "Nobody knows me here. What have I got to lose?" He went forward for healing. He had a major problem with vertigo. When he returned to Glasgow, he noticed that the vertigo had disappeared. Days later he removed the cot he always kept nearby when a vertigo attack came. The vertigo never returned.

God can do anything. The same God who mysteriously put salt into bad water will give you sweet water. The beginning of sweet water, however, is to blame yourself not the world. God does the big things (1 John 1:9); all you do is what these men did: "they brought it to him"— God did the rest.

What happened on Good Friday made no sense at the time, but God was in Christ reconciling the world to Himself. What is going on in your life may make no sense now. Trust an all-wise God to know what He is up to.

And now to the second situation in which God seems to make no sense—what follows I call *respect for the anointing*.

How much respect do you have for the anointing of the Holy Spirit? How much respect do you have for the one who carries that anointing?

This passage—2 Kings 2:23–25—is easy to understand and yet hard to understand. When forty-two young boys are struck dead by the power of God, what are we to believe?

I used to think that Elisha abused his prophetic gift. Did Elisha abuse his anointing? Or was God safeguarding respect for the prophet? Did the Holy Spirit lead Elisha to curse these youths? Or was this Elisha taking their mocking personally—and therefore abusing his anointing? What Elisha did is surely questionable. Would Jesus have reacted like this? Is this what Jesus taught? See Matthew 5:38–39 where Jesus tells us to turn the cheek if we get insulted.

Was Elisha operating under the Law system—"eye for an eye"? If so, he went beyond the Law. Forty-two lads lost their lives!

And yet what happened is not what Elisha did; you have to say that *God did this*. Elisha cursed them in the name of the LORD—that is, Yahweh. God did not have to respond to Elisha's curse. But He did.

Why is this second part of the present chapter important? My reply: it is to teach us respect for the anointing. Anointing is the power of the Holy Spirit; it is the immediate presence of God on deposit in a person approved of God. The presence of the Holy Spirit must be respected, especially when God is pleased to manifest Himself consciously.

For example, in the earliest church, as described especially in the first few chapters of the Book of Acts, there was what I would call a *high level* of the Spirit present. It is my theory that when this exists—which may not happen every day—one must be doubly reverent. What happened with Ananias and Sapphira, who were struck dead when they lied to the Spirit, might not have happened later on. I say this because I suspect there have been those who were not honest before God in the last two thousand years but who were not struck dead. The mistake Ananias and Sapphira made was not discerning the immediate presence of the Spirit. Or perhaps the presence of the Spirit had become so much a part of the church in those days that they did not appreciate it. In any case, both of them lied to Peter about money they claimed to give and were struck dead on the spot.

By the way, there are those who think Peter abused his apostolic authority. Not remotely true. God would never have affirmed what Peter did had not the Spirit led Peter to speak to Ananias and Sapphira as he did. Although there is no biblical injunction that says you have to sell your property and give it to the church, for some reason the Holy Spirit was present in an unusual and unprecedented manner. Lying to an apostle was the issue.

The church in ancient Corinth was in a revival situation. Therefore, when there were those who abused the poor and did not respect the Lord's Supper, God rolled up His sleeves and judged some of them. Some were sick, some were weak, and some died, said Paul (1 Cor. 11:30). By the way, these were saved—not lost—people. For Paul added, "When we are judged by the Lord, we are disciplined so that we may not be condemned along with the world" (1 Cor. 11:32). Indeed, it is *because* people like this are saved that they are judged.

Therefore, this teaching concerning Elisha and children poking fun at him is to teach us respect for God's anointed one—His prophet, His minister. God is no respecter of persons—or age. Strange as it may seem, God esteems His anointing above all else.

> When you were few in number, of little account, and sojourners in it, wandering from nation to nation, from one kingdom to another people, he allowed no one to oppress them; he rebuked kings on their account, saying, "Touch not my anointed ones, do my prophets no harm!"
>
> —1 Chronicles 16:19–22; Psalm 105:12–15

I think this might be a neglected area of study. Many people have abused God's ministers—and seemed to get away with it. I think of passages like these:

> Obey your leaders and submit to them, for they are keeping watch over your souls, as those who will have to give an account. Let them do this with joy and not with groaning, for that would be of no advantage to you.
>
> —Hebrews 13:17

> We ask you, brothers, to respect those who labor among you in the Lord and admonish you, and to esteem them very highly in love because of their work.
>
> —1 Thessalonians 5:12–13

> Let the one who is taught the word share all good things with the one who teaches.
>
> —Galatians 6:6

"Vengeance is mine, I will repay, says the Lord" (Rom. 12:19). God does not always step in immediately. I have a theory: the angrier God is the longer He takes to show it. The imperfection of the minister, prophet, or preacher does not give you a right to speak ill of that person. Elisha was not perfect; it is very possible he should not have done what he did. But God stepped in anyway and defended Elisha, whether it was Elisha personally or the anointing.

An ancient issue in church history was whether the converts who were baptized by ministers who later apostatized needed to be rebaptized. Answer: no. It became the consensus of the church, led partly by St. Augustine, that it was the act of baptism that mattered, not the person who did the baptizing.

So too with the Lord's Supper; it is not the person who administers the bread and wine that matters but the person who partakes of it; they are responsible to discern the Lord's body in the ordinance.

Remember this about any person who has an anointing of the Spirit. They are ordinary people. Very human, very fragile. They were just like you before the anointing came to them; they are still like you but now have a new responsibility. Hopefully it will not go to their heads but they will remain humble. In any case, the anointing on them must be respected.

Paul needed a thorn in the flesh to keep him from being conceited, to keep him from being admired too much (2 Cor. 12:7).

The purpose of the anointing is to demonstrate God's power in an earthen vessel, a jar of clay (2 Cor. 4:7–9). This can be in preaching, especially those with a teaching gift.

The power of the anointing is the power to impart God's Word. Sometimes it's the power to heal. And with Elisha—to his surprise (I am sure)—the power to kill.

What Peter did with Ananias and Sapphira surprised him more than anyone. So too with Elisha when forty-two lads were mauled by bears.

As to the preservation of the anointing, remember that the gifts are without repentance. One does not earn the anointing by being godly. One does not keep it by being godly.

Elisha was given his anointing on one condition: that he see Elijah at the precise moment he was taken up. He made no promise to God. He was granted his request because he saw Elijah taken up.

The protection of the anointing is worth mentioning. Whatever else can be said about Elisha and the killing of the forty-two lads, God had stepped in to protect the anointing. People from that day onward would be very, very careful when it came to a recognized prophet of God.

My advice to all when it comes to respect for the anointing or the anointed: play it safe. David even called Saul "God's anointed" but refused to lay a hand on him (1 Sam. 24:6; 26:9).

CHAPTER 4

GOD'S OVERRULING GRACE

And when the musician played, the hand of the LORD came upon [Elisha]. And he said, "Thus says the LORD, 'I will make this dry streambed full of pools.' For thus says the LORD, 'You shall not see wind or rain, but that streambed shall be filled with water, so that you shall drink, you, your livestock, and your animals.' This is a light thing in the sight of the LORD. He will also give the Moabites into your hand, and you shall attack every fortified city and every choice city, and shall fell every good tree and stop up all springs of water and ruin every good piece of land with stones." The next morning, about the time of offering the sacrifice, behold, water came from the direction of Edom, till the country was filled with water.

—2 KINGS 3:15–20

Music is the art of the prophets and the gift of God.
—MARTIN LUTHER

DO YOU KNOW what it is for God to overrule your plans? Do you know what it is like when God overrules your foolish mistakes?

To overrule means to reject or disallow by exercising one's superior authority. It is when a judge has the official authority to decide against a decision already made, such as when a judge overrules an objection in a court of law, or when the Supreme Court overrules a decision of a lower court.

God is the Supreme overruler. He has the authority to overrule. It is what God does all the time; He works overtime, overruling our mistakes, intervening, stepping in, and letting us save face.

This chapter contains several themes, including (1) how the kings of Israel and Judah turn to Elisha when they are desperate, (2) the ungracious response (at first) of Elisha to these kings, and (3) how God overruled Elisha's somewhat justified bias and unjustified temper.

In the previous chapter we saw how God affirmed Elisha's anointing despite his surprising use of that anointing—cursing some boys for making fun of his bald head.

Elisha may or may not have abused his anointing, but in any case God stepped in despite Elisha apparently losing his temper and sent bears to maul these lads.

In this chapter we look at Elisha's unhelpful comments to Joram, king of Israel. It gives us another glimpse at a prophet's imperfections. Surprising as this may be to some of us, Elisha had a problem with his temper. We must keep in mind both the external anointing and internal anointing. The external may refer to one's public profile—an anointing one keeps. This is irrevocable (Rom. 11:29). There is also the internal—your personal life—fruits of the Spirit such as love, joy, peace, and patience (Gal. 5:22).

One of the purposes of this chapter is to show these

two come together. In short, Elisha's prophetic gift does not kick in until his temper is under control.

> And Jehoshaphat said, "Is there no prophet of the LORD here, through whom we may inquire of the LORD?" Then one of the king of Israel's servants answered, "Elisha the son of Shaphat is here, who poured water on the hands of Elijah." And Jehoshaphat said, "The word of the LORD is with him." So the king of Israel and Jehoshaphat and the king of Edom went down to him. And Elisha said to the king of Israel, "What have I to do with you? Go to the prophets of your father and to the prophets of your mother." But the king of Israel said to him, "No; it is the LORD who has called these three kings to give them into the hand of Moab." And Elisha said, "As the LORD of hosts lives, before whom I stand, were it not that I have regard for Jehoshaphat the king of Judah, I would neither look at you nor see you. But now bring me a musician."
>
> —2 KINGS 3:11–15

Elisha was horrible to the king of Israel (vv. 13–14). There was certainly truth in what Elisha said. But at least Joram was turning to Elisha, even though it was Jehoshaphat's idea to do so.

What follows is how Elisha is unable to help the kings until he calms down. He sends for a harpist. He cools off and God steps in. Music is a gift of common grace. Martin Luther said, "Next to the word of God, music deserves the highest praise."[1]

Once Elisha cools his temper, we see what transpires (vv. 15–16):

> And when the musician played, the hand of the
> LORD came upon him. And he said, "Thus says
> the LORD, 'I will make this dry streambed full of
> pools.'"

The background is this: Moab broke an agreement
with Israel to keep them in lambs and sheep—for food
and clothing. King Joram of Israel decides to attack the
Moabites and asks Jehoshaphat, king of Judah, if he will
join in. The answer: yes (v. 7). But by choosing to go
south and around the Dead Sea they run out of water—
the people and the animals are thirsty. It appears they are
all going to die. Joram thinks that God has determined to
judge them (v. 10).

Jehoshaphat then asks, Is there not a prophet we may
consult? Yes. He is told that a prophet called Elisha who
knew Elijah is around. Joram should have known this, but
it is Jehoshaphat who makes the suggestion. When they
consult Elisha, the prophet turns on Joram (v. 13).

Why is getting a prophetic word important? First, it
is a demonstration of God's overruling grace. The truth
is, God does this *all the time* with us. If it were not for
the overruling grace of God, we would all be undone and
gone long ago. I think of a thousand mistakes I have made.

But I am still here—all owing to God's sheer grace.

Second, it shows how our gift may be of no value unless
our personal life is in order. Whereas Paul said we should
desire earnestly the best or highest gift, the greatest way
to live is by love. He shows this by the great love chapter
of the Bible: 1 Corinthians 13.

Third, this account shows how we may be perfectly
right in our opinion but be completely wrong at the same

time. Elisha had Elijah's anointing. But the anointing did not kick in until Elisha cooled off.

Fourth, it shows how God does not often get our attention until we are utterly desperate. King Joram of Israel would normally never turn to the king of Judah. They had become virtual enemies. Joram would never have turned to Elisha; he was too ashamed to do so.

When things go badly wrong how often the name of God enters into the conversation of wicked people (v. 10).

Fifth, this account in Elisha's life shows how people who are evil still know who their true friends are. Joram knew in his heart that Jehoshaphat would not say no to his request.

Joram also knew that Elisha was the only hope they had.

Sixth, we learn afresh how people in the grip of sin still sense it when God is about to judge them. The wicked Joram sensed that God was judging him by letting Moab defeat all three kings. Joram knew how guilty he was. At least he did not have a seared conscience. "Be sure your sin will find you out" (Num. 32:23).

Seventh, we see how thankful we should be for leaders who know the next wise thing to do. Jehoshaphat, king of Judah, asks: Is there not a prophet? This is the opposite of the proverbial elephant in the room (not talking about the most obvious). Jehoshaphat went straight to the problem: *we need God*. When was the last time a head of state called a nation to a day of prayer and fasting?

Eighth, this passage shows the value of music. Next to theology, said Luther, he loved music. I so agree! Music, as I said, is a gift of God's common grace. You could say that Jubal was the first example (Gen. 4:21).

43

Ninth, this account in 2 Kings 3 demonstrates how quickly God can turn things around.

The next day everything changed; Moab was defeated. I am reminded of how quickly God stepped in during Hezekiah's day. Indeed, "All the people rejoiced because God had provided for the people, *for the thing came about suddenly*" (2 Chron. 29:36, emphasis added).

Tenth, this story is a demonstration of the unpredictable ways of God. The way the kings defeated Moab was not on anybody's radar screen. Water came without rain. The sun shining on the water looked like blood to the Moabites, so they attacked Israel and were utterly defeated. I think this will be true regarding the revival we are praying for. It will take place in a manner nobody would have dreamed of!

Eleventh, this story is a reminder that God is married to the backslider (Jer. 3:14). Israel was part of the ten tribes that broke away years before. The king of Judah might have rejected Joram's request, saying, "That's your problem; you have rejected God"—which is virtually what Elisha said to him. And yet God was still willing to help Israel despite Elisha's first reaction. Could it be that you have wandered far, far from God and yet He comes knocking at your door?

Let us look at Elisha's hasty reaction (vv. 13–14). Elisha spoke before he heard from God, a spontaneous reaction owing to his prejudice. Some people think everything a prophet says is inspired. Wrong. Any prophet has to hear from God or they are as fleshly as any of us. I could tell dozens of stories of some of God's best-known prophetic people of our day. Believe me, they all make mistakes; they are all human.

As to Elisha's hasty reaction, it was unhelpful. He would not win the Nobel Peace Prize for talking like this. Surely this moralizing was unnecessary; it was counterproductive in three ways: (1) It did not help King Joram. (2) It did not help Elisha himself—he grieved the Holy Spirit. It was unfair. After all, wicked though he was, Joram was following Jehoshaphat's advice regarding seeking a prophet. Elisha refused to accept the obvious—that Joram was reaching out because he felt God was turning Israel and Judah over to Moab. (3) It was unnecessary. Before you speak, ask if what you want to say will meet the other person's NEED. Ask yourself:

N—is it necessary to say this?

E—is it energizing? There are two kinds of people: those who drain and those who energize.

E—is it edifying? Does it build them up?

D—is it dignifying? Does it show respect?

Elisha failed on all four of these points!

To Joram's credit (v. 13), he did not cave into Elisha's hasty put-down nor rebuke the prophet but reasoned with him: three kings (Israel, Judah, and Edom) are being judged, and Moab will defeat us all—we have no water, we are desperate. This could obliterate all of us—Israel, Judah, and Edom.

This is when Elisha cooled off and calmed down. But he still had no word yet.

Elisha's request, "Send me a harpist," was a good idea. Why? To cool him off. The right kind of music can do this. A precedent for this may have been set by Samuel. He said to Saul before Saul became king:

> You will meet a group of prophets coming down from the high place with harp, tambourine, flute, and lyre before them, prophesying.
> —1 Samuel 10:5

Young David later played for Saul, who, sadly, became a paranoid king (1 Sam. 16:14–23).

Strange as it may seem, Elisha needed time to calm down in order for his prophetic gift to kick in. I must admit that I understand this. When I am preparing a sermon after an argument with someone, a sense of insight and true meaning of holy Scripture disappears.

Whether they had to dig ditches first—which the NIV and KJV imply—is not certain. Is it what they had to do before God would act? It was fulfilled the next day; they would not have had time to dig ditches. It seems that God did it all without their having to turn a hand. The plan brought relief to those hearing the prophecy.

What is the purpose of prophecy, speaking generally? It is to warn or encourage. This one was to encourage. It was for those needing water so they could survive. This was "an easy thing [for God] to do" (v. 18)—namely, water flowing without rain to precede it. "The next morning, about the time of offering the sacrifice, behold, water came from the direction of Edom, till the country was filled with water" (v. 20).

God has the answer to every problem we can imagine. Their problem: no water.

Do you have a need? Guidance? Healing? Finances?

Wisdom? God always knows the next thing to do. He knows the next step forward. God has unpredictable ways of revealing the next thing for us to do. "Send me a harpist." Whatever is this about? Remember, God's ways are higher than our ways (Isa. 55:8–9); He chooses the foolish things to confound the wise (1 Cor. 1:27). God loves to do what no man or woman would have thought of. He loves to do what is beyond nature, what is miraculous. When it comes to your problem, *think big*. Do not limit God to your own understanding. "Eye has not seen, nor ear heard" what God has prepared for those who love Him and wait for Him (1 Cor. 2:9). We are loved with an everlasting love. God says, "I am married to the backslider." God still loved ancient Israel and even had patience with Joram.

Are you like Joram—some good in you but so much bad? God is on your case.

What if Elisha had not cooled off and not got this changing word from the Lord? All I know is, God overruled. He did it with Elijah; he did it with Elisha.

The best of men are men at best. Though we make stupid mistakes, God is not finished with us yet. He could have rebuked Elisha, but He overruled instead. He could have rebuked Elijah on Carmel for saying, "I alone am left" (he was so wrong), but He overruled instead.

Has God overruled lately in your life? What has happened in your life is for a purpose.

He can turn things around so quickly. God will step in—never too late, never too early, but just on time.

CHAPTER 5

WHEN THE ANSWER IS RIGHT UNDER YOUR NOSE

Now the wife of one of the sons of the prophets cried to Elisha, "Your servant my husband is dead, and you know that your servant feared the LORD, but the creditor has come to take my two children to be his slaves." And Elisha said to her, "What shall I do for you? Tell me; what have you in the house?" And she said, "Your servant has nothing in the house except a jar of oil." Then he said, "Go outside, borrow vessels from all your neighbors, empty vessels and not too few. Then go in and shut the door behind yourself and your son and pour unto all these vessels. And when one is full, set it aside." So she went from him and shut the door behind herself and her sons. And as she poured they brought the vessels to her. When the vessels were full, she said to her son, "Bring me another vessel." And he said to her, "There is not another." Then the oil stopped flowing. She came and told the man of God, and he said, "Go, sell the oil and pay your debts, and you and your sons can live on the rest."

—2 KINGS 4:1–7

> Our faith is not meant to get us out of a hard place or change our painful condition. Rather, it is meant to reveal God's faithfulness to us in the midst of our dire situation.
>
> —David Wilkerson (1931–2011)

ELISHA WAS GIVEN a very wide ministry—as wide as one can imagine. In 2 Kings 3 he deals with heads of states, with kings, with national events. What he did in 2 Kings 3 was to save Israel from starving, defeating the Moabites.

In 2 Kings 4 we find him dealing with an individual person in trouble; the God of the nations is the God of the individual hurting person. It reminds me of a comparison between Acts 2 and Acts 3. In Acts 2 the Gospel reaches thousands. In Acts 3 God shows compassion on one man. But the result is that thousands are saved.

Jesus said that he who is faithful in that which is least is faithful also in much (Luke 16:10).

In 2 Kings 4 Elisha deals with a widow. She was loosely connected with Elisha—the wife of a man from the company of the prophets (v. 1). "You know that he revered the Lord," she says to Elisha. She is, in a way, putting Elisha on the spot, implicitly making a case that she is entitled to something from Elisha. He does not rebuke her. This does show that Elisha knew the man who died. This also shows that the woman was of some stature—she had access to Elisha. It is sometimes helpful to be connected to someone who has access to a sovereign vessel.

Perhaps it is like knowing someone who knows Billy Graham or the Archbishop of Canterbury.

The point is, in 2 Kings 3 Elisha is dealing with nations; in 2 Kings 4:1–7 he is dealing with someone who has a personal problem. She is a widow; her husband was a prophet, although of a low profile. She is having financial problems owing to her husband's death and debts he left behind. "His creditor is coming to take my two boys as his slaves," she says to him.

How do you suppose Elisha responds to this widow? How does God respond to a person who is in desperate circumstances like this? We may think of various options:

- Would God attack the creditor—strike him dead for such ruthlessness? We saw how bears mauled the lads who made fun of Elisha's bald head.

- Would Elisha advise the woman to ask the creditor to be reasonable? Surely it is not right that this creditor would take her two boys to be slaves.

- Would Elisha get people to fast and pray that this ruthless creditor not be so cruel?

- Would Elisha take up an offering to pay this woman's financial obligations?

This story is another example of the unpredictable ways of God. Who could have imagined that God would help this woman in her predicament as Elisha instructed her? Here is what he tells her:

- She is to begin with what she has—a little oil.

- She is to ask people for empty jars—no doubt jars that are useless to the neighbors.

- She is not to ask for money but for items that are not important to the neighbors.

The result: God Himself steps in after she obeys the prophet. She begins with what she has: a little oil. She therefore exhausts her personal resources.

She could have argued, "I need help; that is not going to help me with my problem. What are empty jars going to mean to me?" But she did not complain or question; she respected the wisdom of the prophet although it may have made no sense at the time.

The truth is, the answer was right under her nose!

It is a typical way of how God deals with us. He puts to us a proposition that makes no sense at the time. He said to Abraham that his seed would be as the stars of the Heaven. Lo and behold, Abraham believed God, and his faith counted as righteousness (Gen. 15:6). Later He told Abraham to sacrifice his son Isaac. It made no sense, but Abraham obeyed. As a result, God swore an oath to him. It goes to show that when we trust God in times that make no sense—when God hides His face—He is up to something tremendous!

The greatest example of all of God not making sense is when Jesus, the Son of God, died on a cross. It made no sense. It caught Satan by surprise. It was God's way of overcoming the world and the devil—and saving us from our sins.

Why was this widow required to shut the door before

she could pour oil in the jars? I don't know. Jesus did this just before He raised one from the dead. He asked all to leave (Mark 5:40). Perhaps God does not want us to delve into the miraculous—or the supernatural—but keep our eyes on Him and simply do what He tells us to do.

No one was at the empty tomb when Jesus was resurrected; they discovered that is what happened, but no one saw it as it was happening. So too when Jesus turned water into wine; nobody saw the actual filling of the jars—but they discovered that is what happened (John 2:7–9).

What is the explanation of the oil? How do we know she did not already have enough oil to fill all the jars? Perhaps she had gallons of oil in one large container. Answer: she said that she had "a little oil," so there was not enough to fill several jars. The most striking statement is this, found in verse 6: "the oil stopped flowing." That it "flowed" is a reference to the miraculous. When she used up all the jars "the oil stopped flowing."

The bottom line: God provided her with a way whereby she could make money! He stepped in to do what the widow would not have thought to do. And yet the answer was right under her nose.

She could not manufacture oil. She did what she could with what she had; God did the rest. God did not make money grow on trees. She did not go begging for money; she was told how she could make money and then use it to pay her debts.

This is a reminder of the manna in the desert. It was a miracle food, but it ended when they no longer needed it:

> And the day after the Passover, on that very day,
> they ate of the produce of the land, unleavened cakes

and parched grain. And the manna ceased the day after they ate of the produce of the land. And there was no longer manna for the people of Israel, but they ate of the fruit of the land of Canaan that year.

—JOSHUA 5:11–12

What do we learn from this account?

- God cares about widows (Jas. 1:27).

- We are to use what we have before we ask God for more.

- God cares about our personal finances.

- There is no hint of entitlement in this story. This is a widow; is she not entitled to special treatment? I would have thought so. But there is no giving in to self-pity. She was to learn how she could earn some money.

- The God of miracles teaches us how we can survive when we take what we have and watch Him do the rest.

- God did not want this widow to lose her two children. They were vital to her survival and well-being.

- God cares about families.

- There are ruthless people out there who only care about money and don't care about widows—or single mothers—with young children.

- This is an indication of the depravity of the human heart.

- How could a creditor take two children away from their home? Consider what it would do to the brokenhearted mother, what it would do to the children.

- It is a grim reminder of human slavery in the world today. How could people be so cruel? They think only of money for themselves. Those who sell drugs think only of themselves.

- Mystery: Why would God take a father/husband who reveres the Lord? Why would God take a servant of His when the family so needs him? I have a personal illustration: my own mother died April 8, 1953, aged forty-three; I was seventeen. Why? I don't know.

- The woman got Elisha's attention when she cried. Tears got Elisha's attention. In 2 Kings 20:5 we have the first explicit reference to "tears." Tears got God's attention. Tears got Jesus' attention. He said to the widow who just lost her only son, "Don't cry" (Luke 7:13, NIV). My friend Ernie Reisinger (now in Heaven) told of how a man he worked with—Elmer—had tears in his eyes when he witnessed to Ernie. Tears give us pause.

> He who goes out weeping, bearing the seed for
> sowing, shall come home with shouts of joy, bringing
> his sheaves with him.
>
> —Psalm 126:6

You might say that at the bottom of this entire story is the widow crying. The widow turned to Elisha because she hoped somehow that a man of God would know the next step forward for her. She knew Elisha was in touch with God. He was the only hope she had. Elisha's first response was a question to her, "How can I help?" And then he answered his own question as he thought about it with a question to her: "What do you have in your house?"

How many people would have thought to ask a question like that? Chances are Elisha did not know what his own question would lead to; he was going one step at a time.

Who would have thought "a little oil" would be the solution?

Sometimes what is right under our nose is the next step forward to solving our problem.

This perhaps took a little cheek or boldness for the widow to do: asking neighbors for jars. He also said, "Don't just ask for a few"—a hint right there that Elisha knew where he was going with this. Perhaps Elisha was "fishing" at first; he didn't know what he would find.

Back to the question, Why did she do this after shutting the door behind her and her sons? Just maybe it was for her alone to see God work and know how much He loved her. Or perhaps it was to keep others from seeing how much oil she would end up having—her personal little savings account. What must it have been like pouring oil that was being created before her very eyes? Sometimes God wants to show His power to just one person.

This story demonstrates the dignity of the individual and the dignity of work.

There was no hint of the widow expecting Elisha to give her the money. Many today want a handout; they want everything given to them.

There are injustices in this world. "Life's not fair," said John F. Kennedy (1917–1963). This story in 2 Kings 4 is a perfect example: a widow left with her husband's debts. Then a ruthless creditor takes advantage of her. Some people do get away with murder; people buy off judges; there are starving people, homeless people, people with handicaps, people with diseases, people in constant pain. There are godly people who suffer. Christians are being persecuted in many places in the world. This brings me to Revelation 6:10:

> They cried out with a loud voice, "O Sovereign Lord, holy and true, how long before you will judge and avenge our blood on those who dwell on the earth?"

This account of Elisha shows that people turn to the godly for answers. We must expect the world to turn to us—and we should have answers!

> Always being prepared to make a defense to anyone who asks you for a reason for the hope that is in you.
> —1 PETER 3:15

The most obvious man of God at that time was Elisha. People expect that a man of God will know what to do. What is Elisha supposed to know about a problem like that?

Yes, people will turn to us, however unfairly it may seem, to explain what is going on in the world. We have this promise that when we are called to do so—to heads of state, for example—we take no thought of what to say but trust that God will give us words, as in Matthew 10:20. Although that verse refers to persecuted people having to defend their faith, it shows God's readiness to help us have answers when put on the spot.

Elisha, I think, was fishing for an answer on what to do next by asking the brokenhearted widow, "What *do* you have?"

"A little oil."

God led Elisha one step at a time. Our Lord knows the way through the wilderness; all we have to do is follow.

The answers to our problems are often right under our nose.

What do you have? A little oil? Are you desperate at the moment? Are you at the end of your tether? Could it be that what you have—insignificant though it may seem—is the next step forward in solving your dilemma?

God said to Moses, "What is that in your hand?" Answer: a staff (Exod. 4:2). That staff would be the way through the wilderness. When the Egyptians made one more attempt to defeat the Israelites, God said, "Raise your staff and stretch out your hand over the sea" (Exod. 14:16).

So with Elisha: "Sell your oil and pay your debts, and you and your sons will have enough to live on." No one would have thought of that! This is better than giving the widow money. She did not have to beg. She retained her dignity.

God will do the same for you. What is that in your hand? What do you have? A little oil?

You have a gift that nobody else has. When He made you He threw the mold away. Don't imitate anybody else; God made you as you are with a purpose.

What is under your nose will often take you to the next step. It will take care of you from now on.

CHAPTER 6

WHEN GOD CHOOSES TO SPOIL US

And [Elisha] said, "What then is to be done for her?" Gehazi answered, "Well, she has no son, and her husband is old." He said, "Call her." And when he had called her, she stood in the doorway. And he said, "At this season about this time next year, you shall embrace a son." And she said, "No, my lord, O man of God; do not lie to your servant." But the woman conceived and she bore a son about that time the following spring, as Elisha had said to her.

—2 KINGS 4:14–17

God didn't bless me with success so I could eat caviar every day.

—KATHY LEE GIFFORD

IN THIS PART of the life of Elisha we see another dimension: God is interested in the welfare of rich people. Here we have an example of a wealthy woman who was married to a much older man. She lived in an area where Elisha frequently traveled.

Having stressed in a previous message that we should be content to have our need supplied—and not reach out for comfort or luxury—in this chapter we see that God does give some people comforts if not luxuries. God trusts some of His own with wealth. The Shunammite woman is proof of that. Abraham was wealthy (Gen. 13:2), and so too Joseph of Arimathea (Matt. 27:57). Lydia was a seller of purple (Acts 16:14).

Here is the backdrop for this story:

> One day Elisha went on to Shunem, where a wealthy woman lived, who urged him to eat some food. So whenever he passed that way, he would turn in there to eat food. And she said to her husband, "Behold now, I know that this is a holy man of God who is continually passing our way. Let us make a small room on the roof with walls and put there for him a bed, a table, a chair, and a lamp, so that whenever he comes to us, he can go in there."
>
> One day he came there, and he turned into the chamber and rested there. And he said to Gehazi his servant, "Call this Shunammite." When he had called her, she stood before him. And he said to him, "Say now to her, 'See, you have taken all this trouble for us; what is to be done for you? Would you have a word spoken on your behalf to the king or to the commander of the army?'" She answered, "I dwell among my own people."
>
> —2 KINGS 4:8–13

The persons in this story are the wealthy Shunammite woman and Elisha. Here is what we know about the Shunammite: Not only was she wealthy, but she urged Elisha to come to her home for a meal when he was passing near her. She suggested to her husband that they build a room for Elisha on their roof and provide a bed, lamp, table, and chair for Elisha to use when he was there. She referred to Elisha as a holy man of God. She claimed to dwell among her own people. By that she meant that she did not bother with kings and heads of state for favors. Elisha wanted to know if she wanted any kind of favor. Perhaps someone would say, "Shame on Elisha," for suggesting such a thing. In any case it shows that Elisha had influence in high places; he thought he might take advantage of this for the Shunammite. But no, it was an unintended but timely put-down to Elisha!

It turned out that this woman was childless. Do you know what it is to be childless? Are you childless and want a child?

Elisha prophesied that she would have a son in one year. She replied, "Do not lie to your servant." She was not meaning to be impolite; she did not want to get her hopes up.

Here is what we know about Elisha at this point: he traveled often to Shunem, a town in northern Israel. He would stop when he was in the area to get a meal. One day he went there to rest. He asked his servant, Gehazi, to call the lady. He instructed Gehazi to find out what could be done for her. Should Elisha say a word to the king? Or to the commander of the army? This shows that Elisha had influence in high places. He asked Gehazi again, "What can be done for her?"

Gehazi discovered that the woman had no son and her husband was old. Elisha instructed Gehazi to call her. As she stood in the doorway, he prophesied that she would have a son in one year.

Elisha's prophecy was fulfilled; she bore a son at that time a year later.

Why is this story important? First, it shows that God cares for the poor but also cares for the rich. Furthermore, sometimes God wants to spoil us. He spoiled the Shunammite with wealth. The Shunammite lady spoiled Elisha with what she could do for him.

Rich people may seem to have everything they need, but they don't have everything they want—this childless couple wanted a child.

Second, this story shows a demonstration of mutual gratitude. The Shunammite wanted to show gratitude to Elisha. Elisha wanted to show gratitude to the Shunammite for her kindness to him.

Third, it shows that God is the author of life; He is the one who gives children.

Fourth, this account regarding Elisha shows that God can give life-changing prophecies. It also shows one of the mysteries of prophecies: Elisha could see that the Shunammite woman would have had a baby the following year anyway. Here is an interesting question: *Was* she going to have a baby in any case a year later and Elisha merely tuned in on it, or did his prophecy bring it into being? Or did the prophecy inspire the woman and her husband to believe it could happen?

This story also shows that rich people have a responsibility. They need to be generous givers to the Lord's work. I believe in tithing. All people should tithe. Sadly, my experience is that few rich people tithe. They should be giving above the tithe. They should look to bless godly causes.

Leaders also have a great responsibility, a responsibility not always appreciated. These leaders have to be above reproach. This includes that they must not try to butter up the rich to get favors. Listen to James:

> Not many of you should become teachers, my brothers, for you know that we who teach will be judged with greater strictness. For we all stumble in many ways. And if anyone does not stumble in what he says, he is a perfect man, able also to bridle his whole body.
>
> —JAMES 3:1–2

It is fitting that the Shunammite women of this world should want to do for godly people what they cannot do for themselves. Looking after a minister sometimes shows two extremes: (1) there are those who are afraid they will be too good to their minister; (2) there are those who feel they can't do enough.

The wealthy Shunammite wanted to spoil Elisha. There was nothing wrong with that; God sometimes loves to spoil His children.

Probably the most essential thing we learn from this account is the importance of gratitude. I will never forget as long as I live what happened to me when I was preaching on Philippians 4:6:

> Do not be anxious about anything, but in every-thing by prayer and supplication with thanksgiving let your requests be made known to God.

Right in the middle of my sermon the Holy Spirit convicted me of my own ingratitude. Never in my ministry had anything like this happened to me when preaching—nor since. (I wish it would happen more often.) It was as though my whole life came before me, with God showing me how utterly ungrateful I had been. I went to my vestry after the sermon, fell on my knees, and promised that from that day I would be a thankful man. I can honestly report that it is a vow I have kept.

The psalms are full of praise and gratitude. A Mayo Clinic article claims that a thankful heart increases longevity.[1] Put another way: thankful people live longer. Here is what I know: God loves gratitude; He hates ingratitude. Gratitude (like tithing) must be taught. Ingratitude is listed with the heinous sins of Romans 1. When Jesus healed ten lepers, only one returned to say thank you. His immediate response was, "Where are the nine?" who did not bother to say thank you (Luke 17:17). God notices it when we fail to thank Him.

This story of Elisha and the Shunammite contains another deep teaching: the mystery of prophecy. It is like the old question "Which comes first, the chicken or the egg?" So which comes first, what God had already decided (predestination) or what Elisha prophesied?

I answer: God knows the end from the beginning. Elisha's prophecy did not cause the birth of the son. God had already determined the birth of the son; Elisha was given the privilege of announcing it.

This is true with all prophecy. Prophecy does not make things happen. God determines the end from the beginning:

> For I am God, and there is no other; I am God, and there is none like me, declaring the end from the beginning and from ancient times things not

yet done, saying, "My counsel shall stand, and I will accomplish all my purpose."

—Isaiah 46:9–10

Or as St. Augustine put it: a God who does not know the future is not God. Prophecy is given for basically two reasons: (1) to encourage and (2) to warn. Let me conclude this chapter by pointing out these six important truths:

1. We must not despise prophesying (1 Thess. 5:20).

2. God cares for hurting people—rich or poor.

3. Don't give up praying for what is heavy on your heart.

4. God may want to spoil you. Nothing is impossible with Him.

5. God loves gratitude; He hates ingratitude.

6. The bottom line of all true prophecy is expressed by Paul: "Oh, the depth of the riches and wisdom and knowledge of God! How unsearchable are his judgments and how inscrutable his ways!" (Rom. 11:33).

CHAPTER 7

When Bad Things Happen to Godly People

When Elisha came into the house, he saw the child lying dead on his bed. So he went in and shut the door behind the two of them and prayed to the LORD. Then he went up and lay on the child, putting his mouth on his mouth, his eyes on his eyes, and his hands on his hands. And as he stretched himself upon him, the flesh of the child became warm. Then he got up again and walked once back and forth in the house and went up and stretched himself upon him. The child sneezed seven times, and the child opened his eyes. Then he summoned Gehazi and said, "Call this Shunammite." So he called her. And when she came to him, he said, "Pick up your son." She came and fell at his feet, bowing to the ground. Then she picked up her son and went out.

—2 KINGS 4:32–37

Again I saw that under the sun the race is not to
the swift, nor the battle to the strong, nor bread to
the wise, nor riches to the intelligent, nor favor to
those with knowledge, but time and chance happen
to them all.

—ECCLESIASTES 9:11

There is no erratic power, or action, or motion in
creatures, but that they are governed by God's secret
plan in such a way that nothing happens except what
is knowingly and willingly decreed by Him.

—JOHN CALVIN (1509–1564)

I T IS AN old question: Why do good things happen to
bad people and bad things happen to good people?
This relates to the eternal problem of evil. Why did
God create the world while knowing that humankind
would suffer? I would ask the reader to look at my book
Totally Forgiving God. I will mention one thing in that
book regarding the question of why God allows suffering.
One answer is *so we can have faith.* If you understood why
God allows evil and suffering, you would never need faith.
God has decreed that people "believe" in His Son and the
Gospel by hearing preaching (1 Cor. 1:21). Paul even calls
it the "folly" of what is preached—that people should trust
the blood of Jesus Christ to save them. It seems foolish,
but it is the wisdom of God. We will not always have the
privilege of faith; it is only in this life that we have the
wonderful invitation to believe the Gospel. Everyone will
believe in God after they die.

This chapter is about the Shunammite's child, who

suddenly died and was raised from the dead by Elisha the prophet. Elisha prophesied that the Shunammite would have a son within a year; this prophecy was fulfilled. But the child died. The Shunammite goes to Elisha in haste and brings him to her dead son. Elisha mysteriously lies on top of the boy, and he is revived.

Let's look at the full passage first:

> When the child had grown, he went out one day to his father among the reapers. And he said to his father, "Oh, my head, my head!" The father said to his servant, "Carry him to his mother." And when he had lifted him, and brought him to his mother, the child sat on her lap till noon, and then he died. And she went up and laid him on the bed of the man of God and shut the door behind him and went out. Then she called to her husband and said, "Send me one of the servants and one of the donkeys, that I may quickly go to the man of God and come back again." And he said, "Why will you go to him today? It is neither new moon nor Sabbath." She said, "All is well." Then she saddled the donkey, and she said to her servant, "Urge the animal on; do not slacken the pace for me unless I tell you." So she set out and came to the man of God at Mount Carmel.
>
> When the man of God saw her coming, he said to Gehazi his servant, "Look, there is the Shunammite. Run at once to meet her and say to her, 'Is all well with you? Is all well with your husband? Is all well with the child?'" and she answered, "All is well." And when she came to the mountain to the man of God, she caught hold of his feet. And

Gehazi came to push her away. But the man of God said, "Leave her alone, for she is in bitter distress, and the LORD has hidden it from me and has not told me." Then she said, "Did I ask my lord for a son? Did I not say, 'Do not deceive me?'" He said to Gehazi, "Tie up your garment and take my staff in your hand and go. If you meet anyone, do not greet him, and if anyone greets you, do not reply. And lay my staff on the face of the child." Then the mother of the child said, "As the LORD lives and as you yourself live, I will not leave you." So he arose and followed her. Gehazi went on ahead and laid the staff on the face of the child, but there was no sound or sign of life. Therefore he returned to meet him and told him, "The child has not awakened."

When Elisha came into the house, he saw the child lying dead on his bed. So he went in and shut the door behind the two of them and prayed to the LORD. Then he went up and lay on the child, putting his mouth on his mouth, his eyes on his eyes, and his hands on his hands. And as he stretched himself upon him, the flesh of the child became warm. Then he got up again and walked once back and forth in the house and went up and stretched himself upon him. The child sneezed seven times, and the child opened his eyes. Then he summoned Gehazi and said, "Call this Shunammite." So he called her. And when she came to him, he said, "Pick up your son." She came and fell at his feet, bowing to the ground. Then she picked up her son and went out.

—2 KINGS 4:18–37

Why is this chapter important? It demonstrates several things. First, we will examine the predicament that followed the promised child suddenly being taken away. All that the mother could think of was getting Elisha involved. Puzzles emerge in this story; there are several things that are hard to understand. Second, this gives us a glimpse into the typical pain of a prophet. Most people have never thought about this. I know I didn't—that is, until I got up close to some prophetic people and saw the torture they go through when people turn on them. Third, you may have wished for a prophetic gift, but when you see what a prophet often goes through, you might reassess your desire. This story shows how a prophet is put on the spot and how people want to hold that prophet liable for the way things turn out. We who were so glad to get a reliable "word" from a prophet are also the first to say, "What are you going to do about this?," when things take an unexpected turn.

A prophetic person learns to beware of giving people a word; they will almost always want an elaboration a little bit later. We are all insatiable when it comes to this sort of thing. We want more and more information. Why don't they tell us more? People somehow think prophetic ministers are supposed to explain why and when certain things will happen—or not happen!

Life is full of mysteries. Some predicaments end well; some do not.

The account in this chapter ended well.

Could there be someone reading these lines who is in the middle of a crisis right now; you don't know how it will end. Not all predicaments end well—even for godly people. There are times when God appears to betray us.

All those described in Hebrews 11 broke the "betrayal barrier." That means there were times in their lives in which they felt betrayed by God—that God let them down. Martin Luther taught that you must know God as an enemy before you can know Him as a friend. Almost all sovereign vessels sooner or later experience the betrayal barrier. At some time along the way God seems like an enemy, working against us instead of for us. This is the way Habakkuk felt (Hab. 1:13).

Let us look at the predicament—a difficult, unpleasant, or embarrassing situation. Elisha prophesied that this lady would have a child. She had not asked for a word from him. He volunteered this. Her immediate worry emerged when he gave it: "Don't get my hopes up." The prophecy was fulfilled just as Elisha said. But after a while the same child suddenly died. The first thing the Shunammite woman said to Elisha was, "Didn't I tell you, 'Don't raise my hopes'?"

She was angry with Elisha and wanted to hold him responsible, although he had done nothing wrong. She somehow felt entitled either to an explanation or to Elisha putting this right—as if this were his responsibility. The Shunammite fell into the trap we all face: a sense of entitlement. When things go wrong, we want to blame God. Sometimes a feeling of entitlement comes from a faulty theology, as if God owes us something. It emerges from the belief that we are entitled to all good things, whether from God, from the government, or from people. This is individualism to an extreme. It is part of the "me" generation, the "What's in it for me?" era. The truth is no one is entitled; we are at the Lord's mercy in everything.

Be willing to wait, work, and worship the God who does not have to answer at our beck and call.

In a word, the Shunammite felt entitled to an explanation. She had been gracious to Elisha, giving him a room and good food whenever he asked for it—all her idea. So Elisha felt that he should show his gratitude to her and gave her a prophetic word she did not expect—or believe! But his word came true. And yet it was not Elisha's responsibility to sort things out after the child died.

Perhaps Elisha wished he had never given her the prophetic word. Perhaps he should have accepted her generosity without feeling a need to pay her back. It is a sobering reminder that there is often a downside to every relationship. Indeed many relationships that started out brilliantly later turn sour. Frankly, I have had this happen more than I care to think about.

Are you in a predicament at the moment? Perhaps God promised you a job; you get it but then get laid off. Perhaps God promised that you would get healed, but you get sick again. Maybe God promised you a better place to live; you get it, but things fall apart after you have the new home. Possibly God promised you that you would find a spouse, but the marriage breaks down.

It is a natural instinct to feel God owes us an explanation. We feel entitled for God to sort things out.

What if He does sort things out? What if He doesn't? How are we to cope with situations like this?

This part of the Elisha story is full of puzzles. Why did God give the Shunammite a son then take him away? What is the point about new moons or Sabbaths? Why did she say, "Everything is all right," when things were certainly not all right. Why didn't the Lord show Elisha why the woman was in distress? He himself did not know until she told him. It shows that a prophet doesn't know everything! And why did Elisha lie on top of the boy mouth-to-mouth, eye-to-eye?

I will not try to answer these questions. Life is full of mysteries. A new Christian is almost always plunged into unexplainable suffering after they are truly converted. They may have imagined that being a Christian would solve all their problems. No minister, no evangelist, nor pastor or teacher thought to warn them that extremely difficult problems would come up. We all have so many questions we want answered. I have a prayer list that includes mentioning verses in the Bible I don't understand! There are riddles: Why did God do this and not that? What do difficult verses mean? Why are there things in the Bible that are impossible for many of us to grasp? For example, why is there a Hell? If God does not want people to go to Hell, why doesn't He destroy Hell itself? Why did He create it?

The Shunammite was in pain—she lost her one and only son, the one who came by a prophetic promise. As I said, this story shows the pain of Elisha, how he is implicitly blamed and unjustly carries the responsibility for the child's death. The truth is that the Shunammite loved Elisha; he loved her. But she had no one else to turn to. He knew that. He did not rebuke her or say, "That's not my problem."

While writing this book I came down with a fever. I talked to a person who has an undoubted prophetic gift. Many of his prophecies—and their fulfillments—are absolutely amazing. I phoned him when I had a high temperature and asked him to pray for me. He said, "You don't have COVID." That was a relief. But my physician persuaded Louise and me to get tested to be sure. We both tested positive. Both of us had COVID. I didn't want to tell him, but he asked me. The fact that Paul said we should "despise not prophesyings" (KJV) but immediately added "prove all things" is a dead giveaway that not all prophecies will be accurate. The problem is—dare I say it—all of Elijah's and Elisha's prophecies were absolutely accurate. First Thessalonians 5:20–21 shows that New Testament prophets do not necessarily have the same authority as those in the Old Testament era. Indeed theologian Wayne Grudem has shown convincingly that the Old Testament prophet was succeeded by the New Testament apostles and that the admonitions to prophesy (1 Cor. 14:1) are not meant to encourage you and me to think we can be Elishas!

As for Elisha, he was most anxious to come to the Shunammite's rescue. Some things remain a mystery: Why did Elisha not know that the Shunammite's son had died? It would seem reasonable to think that God would tell him first. But no. Why did his staff not heal the dead son, as Elisha instructed Gehazi? Why did Elisha have to do what appears to be mouth-to-mouth resuscitation before the child was raised to life? Some things are obviously meant to remain a mystery. The same kind of question could be asked about Jesus' various ways of healing people. Some were healed by remote control, others when He was physically present.

I appeal to Isaiah:

> For my thoughts are not your thoughts, neither are your ways my ways, declares the LORD. For as the heavens are higher than the earth, so are my ways

higher than your ways and my thoughts than your
thoughts.

—Isaiah 55:8–9

What is an intelligent, reasonable, sensible, and honest
person to do? I answer: *you choose to believe the Bible
without getting all your questions answered.*

There are parentheses in the story, in verse 26, with
three questions: (1) Are you all right? (2) Is your husband
all right? (3) Is your child all right? Elisha asked these
questions because he didn't know the answers.

And yet this story demonstrates how God knows what
we are going through.

Nothing is hidden from Him (Heb. 4:13). In this world
we will have trouble. Jesus promised this (John 16:33).
Away with foolish people who make the claim that all of
us should always have victory, get all our prayers answered,
and always be healed—that if it is not good it is from the
devil! Such teaching is utter nonsense, and these people
have a lot to answer for. Such exposure has already begun.

This life is not all there is. We are on our way to
Heaven. It is *there* where there will be no suffering or
crying (Rev. 21:4).

When God seems to betray you, *congratulations*! A
valid—if not the best—translation of the Greek word
makarios, translated "blessed," is "congratulations."
"Blessed are those who mourn, for they shall be com-
forted" (Matt. 5:4): congratulations. Are you persecuted
(Matt. 5:11)? Congratulations! You have been promoted
to the big leagues. God has a special plan for you. Bad
things happen to godly people.

But it ain't over till it's over.

CHAPTER 8

Death in the Pot

And Elisha came again to Gilgal when there was a famine in the land. And as the sons of the prophets were sitting before him, he said to his servant, "Set on the large pot, and boil stew for the sons of the prophets." One of them went out into the field to gather herbs, and found a wild vine and gathered from it his lap full of wild gourds, and came and cut them up into the pot of stew, not knowing what they were. And they poured out some for the men to eat. But while they were eating of the stew, they cried out, "O man of God, there is death in the pot!" And they could not eat it. He said, "Then bring flour." And he threw it into the pot and said, "Pour some out for the men, that they may eat." And there was no harm in the pot.

—2 Kings 4:38–41

An unholy church! It is useless to the world, and of no esteem among men. It is an abomination, Hell's laughter, Heaven's abhorrence. The worst evils which have ever come upon the world have been brought upon her by an unholy church.

—Charles H. Spurgeon

THIS ACCOUNT CONTAINS another of Elisha's miracles. There is a famine in the region, and a group of prophets have met to be instructed by Elisha, their mentor. He apparently is responsible for feeding them. One of the prophets, meaning to be helpful, gathers some herbs and wild gourds, cuts them up, and puts them in the stew Elisha orders to be prepared. As soon as the prophets taste it they exclaim, "There's death in the pot!" Elisha does not panic but has flour put into the pot; they all eat it without any harm.

There are two ways of dealing with this incident in Elisha's life and ministry. The first would be to treat the account historically, to show that as Elisha put salt on water to make it pure, so too he puts flour in the poisonous soup to make it harmless. There was a famine in the area of Gilgal, but, so it would seem, not of hearing the word of the Lord with Elisha and these prophets around. It is wonderful when there is a hearing of the word of the Lord. We must not take this for granted; there are places in the world that would love to have a ministry of the Word and where the Gospel would be preached. We must pray for more Gospel preaching—that God will spread the Word and the numbers of believers will increase!

Gilgal was a special spot for Elisha. Whereas God's presence is everywhere, there are to all of us special places. Elisha's school of the prophets became the name Charles Spurgeon would use for his school in which he sought to train ministers for preaching the Gospel.

What was death in the pot? It was a bit of poison that would kill if swallowed. Matthew Henry said of these prophets that they "knew their Bibles but not their herbals." Their taste buds were good; otherwise, they would have died from the stew. The reference to "sons of the prophets" brings up the question of whether the gift of prophecy can be inherited. There is apparently something hereditary about some prophets. Amos said that he himself was not a prophet nor the son of a prophet (Amos 7:14). The late Paul Cain (1929–2019), whom I knew well, often spoke of his mother and grandmother, who were quite prophetic.

It is interesting that Elisha does not suggest they throw out the bad stew but rather that they add something to the stew—flour—to heal it. As salt had cured the impure water in a previous miracle, so flour—some versions say meal—was added. The stew was now safe to eat.

We now turn to a second way of looking at this miracle— its prophetic or allegorical significance. This is the way this passage has often been applied. There was nothing about the appearance of the stew that looked dangerous. Sometimes a food can look appetizing and delicious, especially if you are hungry. But if swallowed it can lead to illness from food poisoning—or even death. The spiritual equivalent is to taste what is different, or strange; if not recognized it can lead to spiritual poisoning that can be fatally damaging.

From this we may learn how good people can partake of something innocent but it can be dangerous if not detected in time. It requires that our "spiritual taste buds" be sharp and able to detect what would be bad. "The little foxes spoil the vines" (Song 2:15). It is like a plane leaving New York for London that gets off track by a minute degree. If not detected, the plane will be circling around Spain rather than London six hours later.

For example, I have warned a lot of people recently of the danger of a teaching called open theism. Some listen to me, some don't. It springs from the idea that God wants our input in order to know what He should do. It is based on the notion that (1) God does not know the future but only the present and (2) does not have a will of His own but is dependent on our cooperation with Him in order to know what His will is. This teaching is dangerous. It is actually sub-Christian. But it has taken millions by storm although most do not even know the term *open theism*.

Open theism is an example of "death in the pot." It is in many seminaries. It is held on to by liberals but also those who have been Evangelicals. Whereas it is a common theology among liberals, there are those who believe in the virgin birth and resurrection of Jesus who have embraced open theism without knowing it. Well-known preachers, scholars, and theologians are teaching this. Open theism is within a hair's breadth of atheism and virtually the same as pantheism.

The "name it and claim it" teaching springs from this kind of thinking. Those who propagate it teach that we are to *claim what we want and hold to it*—we force God to do what we tell Him. This teaching is bent on changing God's will rather than finding out what His will is. It is totally man-centered and has eliminated any possibility of belief in the sovereignty of God.

In the 1960s a well-known Southern Baptist aptly warned of those who taught that the first eleven chapters of Genesis are not historical. He warned of this because some seminary professors were teaching that the Garden of Eden was not a place on the map; neither was the fall of man a date in history. He preached a famous sermon that he called "Death in the Pot."

I am doing my best to teach and preach this in the days

I have left on earth to minister—whether to Word people or Spirit people, whether to Charismatics or Evangelicals. I cry with all my heart for people to recognize "death in the pot." It leads to what Charles Spurgeon called "an unholy church." Even at the natural level we must watch what we eat, what we drink, what we watch on TV; we must guard our entertainment and the music we listen to. We should be able to get just a "sip" or small "bite" of something and know whether to proceed. The prophets caught the poisonous stew in the nick of time. In my own life, I am thankful that I was spared from imbibing liberal teaching—neoorthodoxy, Barthianism, open theism, and such teachings—having had a "taste." It has enabled me to develop a theological radar that can spot heresy when it emerges.

What is interesting but not necessarily easy to apply is how God chose to deal with the negative situation in Gilgal at this dinner for the prophets. He did not deal with an extreme negative negatively. What I mean is this. Elisha did not have the men throw out the stew but rather add something to it. Flour. Meal. If I may apply this personally, I really do thank God for my education. I learned what I could from the most liberal professors at my old seminary—strange as it may seem. Some of the most liberal of them put me in Oxford. Had I been negative and faultfinding I might have won the battle but lost the war.

When it comes to those in our day whose theology we oppose, we must love them, pray for them, and thank God for the good they truly do. Let us put flour in the pot.

Is there an equivalent of "death in the pot" other than what is theological? Yes. In the church when there is a falling into sin—or grumbling, a rival spirit, jealousy, lack of commitment, and unforgiveness—we must be tender with people. If we believe someone is overtaken in a sin like these, we must do what we can to restore such a person in the spirit of deep humility, considering our own weakness lest we be next to fall into sin (Gal. 6:1).

In your home if there is unfaithfulness, holding grudges, keeping a record of wrongs, lack of a consistent prayer life and reading your Bible, or carelessness with money, throw "flour"—patience—instead of harsh criticism.

In your marriage if there is a constant pointing of the finger, keeping a record of wrongs, or complaining, try tearing up the "record of wrongs" (1 Cor. 13:5). When there is death in the pot, get help. It may mean that you seek counseling. I did for a number of months when at Westminster Chapel. Our marriage was under a strain. We sought help. It made a difference.

How do you deal with "death in the pot"? My advice: unless God steps in sovereignly on His own, try love. Tenderness. Compassion. Understanding. "Every person is worth understanding," said Clyde Narramore (1916-2015).

Ask yourself this question: Do we want God to send judgment? Or do we want revival? Hope and pray for the latter.

CHAPTER 9

THE NEW AND
DIFFERENT

A man came from Baal-shalishah, bringing the man of God bread of the firstfruits, twenty loaves of barley and fresh ears of grain in his sack. And Elisha said, "Give to the men, that they may eat." But his servant said, "How can I set this before a hundred men?" So he repeated, "Give them to the men, that they may eat, for thus says the LORD, 'They shall eat and have some left.'" So he set it before them. And they ate and had some left, according to the word of the LORD.

—2 KINGS 4:42–44

And if you say in your heart, "How may we know the word that the LORD has not spoken?"—when a prophet speaks in the name of the LORD, if the word does not come to pass or come true, that is a word that the LORD has not spoken; the prophet has spoken it presumptuously. You need not be afraid of him.

—DEUTERONOMY 18:21–22

Two roads diverged in a wood, and I—I took the road less traveled by,
And that has made all the difference.

—ROBERT FROST (1874–1963)

I USED TO BE a door-to-door vacuum cleaner salesman. My line to get into someone's home to give a demonstration of my product was, "I've come to show you something new and different for your home." The notion of new and different appealed to some people.

Are you open to the new and different? Or only to the old and same?

This chapter deals with another miracle in the life of Elisha, an extension in fact of the previous account regarding "Death in the Pot." Chances are this was part of the same occasion—lasting for more than one day— concerning the one hundred prophets. Someone probably brought more food to feed the prophets during their time together. The problem, however, was that there wasn't enough of the donated food to feed one hundred men.

Although there was not nearly enough food, Elisha stepped in and commanded them to eat what was there. He prophesied: "They shall eat and have some left." This was a bold pronouncement, unprecedented in biblical history. Hundreds of years later Jesus performed the same kind of miracle twice (Matt. 14:13–21; 15:32–39), but this was new and different when Elisha did what he did. Whereas in Moses' day the children of Israel were fed with supernatural food, called "manna" (Exod. 16:15–21), there was no precedent for natural food being multiplied. This bold prophecy was fulfilled: "They ate and had some left, according to the word of the Lord" (2 Kings 4:44).

I heard missionary Heidi Baker tell an amazing story; she and her husband, Rolland, witnessed virtually the same thing in Mozambique. They invited a dozen people to their home for dinner. Forty turned up! What were they going to do? They watched God multiply the food as they ate, and all had enough to eat.

Elisha felt responsible to feed the one hundred men; he was the leader of these prophets. Some have compared this to a Bible college, with Elisha the head teacher.

Elisha's word and "word of the LORD" are the same on this occasion. Elisha said, "Thus says the LORD, 'They shall eat and have some left.'" It is written: "They ate and had some left, according to the word of the LORD."

Both Elisha and Elijah were extraordinarily human. James specifically emphasized that about Elijah (Jas. 5:17). He could have said it about Elisha. As for Elijah, not all that he said was true. When he said, "I alone am left," he was wrong. See 1 Kings 18:22, 19:10, and Romans 11:3–4. When Elisha gave a pronouncement—at least on this occasion—it was elevated to being the very word of God. When Elisha said, "The LORD says," it was owned by the Lord.

I have urged people wherever I go: *don't say things like this*. Who says you have the right to claim you are the equivalent of Elisha?

The man from Baal-shalishah brought "bread of the firstfruits" (2 Kings 4:42). This refers to the *tithe*! What this man did was tithe from his own land. The tithe is one-tenth. He was honoring God and regarded bringing the tithe from his land to Elisha's school of the prophets as giving to God. Malachi said that God will honor those who pay their tithe by blessing so that "there will not be room enough to store it" (Mal. 3:10, NIV). One could easily deduce that God was honoring not only Elisha's word but also honoring this man's tithe.

Abraham was the first tither. He was doing something that was new and different. What he did was voluntary, spontaneous. How did he know to tithe? It was the Holy Spirit preparing the people of God for how His work should be supported. While Abraham's tithe was voluntary and spontaneous, Moses—who brought the Law four hundred years later—made it mandatory. Even Malachi, writing during the parenthetical thirteen-hundred-year era of the Law, says that we cannot "out-give" the Lord. Paul confirmed this:

> Whoever sows sparingly will also reap sparingly, and whoever sows bountifully will also reap bountifully.
> —2 CORINTHIANS 9:6

By the way, when someone says, "It ain't the money, it's the principle," it's the money. Elisha affirms the man's tithe by his infallible prophecy.

It was a new miracle. Unprecedented. Never in the history of Israel had there been a miracle like this. Some of the miracles done by Elisha had a precedent in Elijah. But a miracle of food being multiplied had never been done before.

Are you open to the new? To the different? This is often more of a personality issue than a spiritual issue. Some people are just congenitally opposed to anything unprecedented. It is the way they are wired. Many of us are like that. We don't want to move out of our comfort zones. The greatest risk of my whole ministry was having Arthur Blessitt, the man who carried a cross around the world (and listed in Guinness World Records for the world's longest walk), at Westminster Chapel. He turned us upside down, but it was the best decision I made in my twenty-five years there. Believe me, I went right out of my comfort zone! But I never have been sorry.

Elisha's servant's reaction was predictable: "How can I set twenty loaves of bread before a hundred men?" What if God wants to work in your life and do what has never been done before? And what if you are the only one given this mandate?

It was a noble miracle. The man from Baal-shalishah not only gave his tithe to Elisha; Elisha shared it with the one hundred men. Elisha might have said to his servant, "Let's keep some of this and these ears of grain to ourselves; why give it to these one hundred men?" No, they did not keep a bit of it to themselves; they gave it all away. Elisha gave what was his, but he did not see it as his. Remember: the tithe is God's money. How you handle God's money is something God notices—even if we are not aware of it.

It was a needful miracle. These men had to eat. God chose to feed them in the middle of a famine. God does not do gratuitous miracles! That is what King Herod wanted—for Jesus to perform a miracle like a magician would do (Luke 23:8).

God knows we need to eat. We should pray the Lord's Prayer daily: "Give us this day our daily bread" (Matt. 6:11). This prayer should also make us aware of people who don't have food.

It was a nutritious miracle. What God provided was not only tasty but good for them. God does not provide sustenance that is not good for us!

Why is this story important?

First, it anticipates the miracle of Jesus feeding the five thousand with loaves and fish. Elisha's miracle hardly compares to Jesus feeding five thousand. But it was certainly unprecedented.

Second, it shows an unprecedented way in which God can manifest His power. God can repeat Himself; often He does what is unprecedented.

When people criticize something for which there is no biblical precedent, it is often because they don't want to come out of their comfort zones. There is not a precedent (that I know of) for carrying a man-made wooden cross around the world as Arthur Blessitt has done. I point people to Hebrews 11, the faith chapter of the Bible. Not a single person mentioned had the advantage of repeating what a person of faith had done previously. Enoch walked with God and was translated to Heaven (Heb. 11:5). Noah walked with God but was required to build an ark (Heb. 11:7). Abraham walked with God and did not know where he was going (Heb. 11:8)! None had the privilege of repeating what had been done before.

Third, this story is important because it shows that prophets need teaching. This would be the reason these one hundred men met. It is impossible to know how Elijah was taught before he appeared on the scene out of the blue (1 Kings 17:1). But his knowledge of the "God of Israel" shows he was taught. It is impossible to know how much Elisha learned from Elijah and how much came from immediate and direct knowledge from God Himself. It is impossible to know what Elisha actually taught these one hundred prophets. But they obviously needed teaching, and it is apparent Elisha was qualified.

Fourth, this story shows that men of God need to be fed; they need to eat! No one is so godly or spiritual that they outgrow needing to eat. Godly people also need to watch their intake and quality of food too. Never forget that people who preach the Gospel live from the financial help of those who uphold this Gospel (1 Cor. 9:14; 1 Tim. 5:17–18). We learn therefore that the Elishas of this world depend on people to support them financially.

Fifth, only a person with an extremely high level of anointing would dare promise what Elisha promised. After all, in an hour or two all would know! When there is a "thus says the Lord" attached, you had better be absolutely, undoubtedly, and categorically sure God told you to say that. In light of Jesus' explanation of the third commandment (Matt. 5:33–37) not to misuse the name of the Lord, I seriously doubt if God leads *anyone* to say, "Thus says the Lord," nowadays. Those amateurs today—and some not so amateur—who use the phrase "Thus says the Lord" or "The Lord told me" are, in my opinion, being very foolish.

There is no need to bring in the Lord's name, no need to say that when the authority is so obvious. Sadly, it is often those whose prophetic utterance is in doubt who say, "Thus says the Lord." They do it not to make God look good but to enhance their own respectability and credibility. Furthermore, when prophetic people get it wrong after claiming to speak for God, they are—in any case—not to be respected (Deut. 18:21–22).

CHAPTER 10

IF ONLY

Now Naaman was commander of the army of the king of Aram. He was a great man in the sight of his master and highly regarded, because through him the Lord had given victory to Aram. He was a valiant soldier, but he had leprosy. Now bands of raiders from Aram had gone out and taken captive a young girl from Israel, and she served Naaman's wife. She said to her mistress, "If only my master would see the prophet who is in Samaria! He would cure him of leprosy." Naaman went to his master and told him what the girl from Israel had said. "By all means, go," the king of Aram replied. "I will send a letter to the king of Israel." So Naaman left, taking with him ten talents of silver, six thousand shekels of gold and ten sets of clothing.

—2 Kings 5:1–5 (niv)

If you only knew what God had to take me through to get me to the place where He could use me to be a blessing to other people, I doubt whether you would be willing to pay the price.

—Charles Swindoll

"IF ONLY" is often regarded as the saddest phrase in the English language. When we think of the phrase "if only," the implication is often negative. For example, "If only these two people could have met sooner," "If only this had happened yesterday," or, when Jesus wept over Jerusalem, "If only you had known what would bring you peace" (Luke 19:42).

But 2 Kings 5:1–5 shows how "if only" ends up in a positive result: the Israeli girl said to her mistress, "If only my master would see the prophet who is in Samaria! He would cure him of his leprosy" (v. 3).

The healing of Naaman from leprosy is one of the most interesting and unusual stories in the entire Old Testament and accounts in the life of Elisha. Naaman was a high-ranking military officer in the army of the king of Aram—now Syria, an enemy of Israel, but there was peace at the time. Remember then that Naaman was not an Israelite, not an heir of the covenant God made with Israel. If anything, Naaman could be regarded as an enemy of Israel. And yet the Word of God says that the *Lord*—that is, the God of Israel—gave Naaman the victory over Israel. It does not say that Syria's god gave victory. It says that the God of Israel gave Naaman the victory over Israel.

Had the God of Israel turned against Israel? For a while, yes. This is the way we should see all wars and all battles. It is not the god of Syria, Baal, or any other deity, but the *Lord* who gives a nation a victory. It is the Lord God of Israel, the God of the Bible, who rules the nations.

The issue therefore becomes this: how do we in this day of pluralism identify the true God? In ancient times they would say "God of Israel"—end of story. Full stop. Can we say this today? Some might. Or would we say the

God of Great Britain? Or the God of the United States of America? Or the God of the Bible Belt?

The answer is, the God of the Bible. That is the best way I know to identify the true God—the Father of our Lord Jesus Christ. In this passage we find the true God at work; here it was the God of Israel.

In any case, God was at work in a surprising place—Syria—where Aleppo is today, the place where the Syrian civil war took place only a few years ago. It cost the former governor of New Mexico his standing in a presidential election; he did not know where Aleppo was.

Here it is called Aram. God was at work there in approximately the eighth century BC—the last place where you would expect for God to be at work. But the unfolding miracle of 2 Kings 5:1–5 took place in Aram. This much you can be sure of about the God of the Bible: "nothing is too difficult for Him," as the chorus goes.

Naaman was a friend of the king, a man of considerable standing. He was a very wealthy man as well. But he had leprosy. When it comes to illness and disease, such things are no respecter of persons. It is true that wealthy people get the best health care; they can purchase the best foods and afford the best vitamins and supplements. But they're not immune to ill health. So too Naaman: his friendship with the king could not heal him. His standing could not heal him. His wealth was of no value. His future was bleak.

There emerges in this story a *surprising peacemaker.* She was a nameless person, a "young girl from Israel" who served Naaman's wife. The unsung hero of the story: a nameless girl from Israel. Most of us like to hear our names mentioned. We are all wired in such a way that we want significance. Jesus said to rejoice that your "names" are written in Heaven (Luke 10:20).

But there is no name given to this young girl. She is a nameless peacemaker. "Blessed are the peacemakers, for they shall be called children of God" (Matt. 5:9). Peacemaking is what she was doing; she was hoping to bring peace to her mistress's husband. But what she had in mind could help bring reconciliation to two nations that had been at war. The stakes were huge—all from this nameless young girl from Israel. She was the least likely to be a person of influence. In those days women had minimal significance, not to mention a young girl. She was an Israelite girl. You could call her an enemy. She was from the very Israel that Aram had just fought and against whom they won a huge battle. You would expect she would work against Naaman, but she became the slave girl of Naaman's wife.

She was submissive. She could easily have been bitter, but she submitted to the Lord's will. She spoke up when she could have been silent, but she spoke a word to her mistress that would result in what was one of the most stupendous miracles in all biblical history.

She was selfless—she never called attention to herself. She was sure—she spoke from experience and had reason to know firsthand what Elisha could do. She was unashamed of God's prophet Elisha.

Had she turned her back on Israel and sided with the enemy? No. She had compassion for her master. Though held captive in Syria, she knew who could help.

By the way, you are a witness in a godless world; you know who can help! Do you tell people about Jesus?

She was a foreigner. Some of the greatest missionaries

of our time are Koreans sent to America and Great Britain. She was a peacemaker. The greatest peacemaker in the world is one who leads a person to peace with God. Being a peacemaker can bring one to be in the most precarious position imaginable: trying to bring two sides together. Both can turn against you.

But this nameless girl is unashamed. She is unsophisticated. She is a nobody; her name would not appear in society columns. She had no pedigree. No references. She was unconnected to those with influence. The heroes in Heaven will be people you never heard of. Rewards at the judgment seat of Christ will be meted out to millions of nameless people.

This story comes into its own by the servant girl's surprising proposal (v. 3). "If only my master would see the prophet who is in Samaria! He would cure him of his leprosy." You could say that this proposal was far-fetched. Out of the blue this nameless servant girl comes with a stunning proposition: "If only my master would see the prophet who is in Samaria! He would cure him of his leprosy." And yet she was fearless. How dare this Israelite girl speak of a prophet in Israel! Imagine this—speaking of a prophet in a hated nation!

It was a faith proposal: he would get cured. It shows that this girl completely won the confidence of her mistress. She had developed a relationship that reflected integrity and high credibility.

Who would have thought it? But Naaman's wife told her husband about her slave girl's proposition. He might have dismissed it out of hand. But we read that *Naaman went to the king*. What persuaded Naaman? And then, lo and behold, the king himself said yes, go. Why then was

Naaman persuaded? Why was the king persuaded? Such a word coming from a nobody, a nameless person with no pedigree, no background.

Why? They were desperate. They had nothing to lose. No one else had a plan. The servant girl's message was unique. It had a ring of authority, of authenticity.

When Joseph spoke to the Pharaoh to save up for the next seven years, it had a ring of authority (Gen. 41:37–38). In the same way our Gospel has the same hope. Paul could say, "I am not ashamed of the gospel" (Rom. 1:16). What pedigree did Paul have? None that would have impressed Romans. What pedigree did Paul have that would have impressed the Corinthians when he said that he determined to know nothing among them except Jesus Christ and Him crucified (1 Cor. 2:2)? From this message came a large church and the largest correspondence to a church in the New Testament.

Are you a nobody? Your word could reach the highest places when you are bold, authentic, and unashamed.

Imagine this: the king of Aram writing a letter to the king of Israel. If you were to guess who was behind this, you would say it must be a person of influence, of high learning, of high ranking, and well-connected.

But no. It was a servant girl with no connections; she just knew what could happen "if only." "If only" normally ends up with negative conclusions and feelings of dismay.

But not this one. Not with our Gospel. When God is at work. When the time is right.

CHAPTER 11

STRANGE WISDOM

But when Elisha the man of God heard that the king of Israel had torn his clothes, he sent to the king, saying, "Why have you torn your clothes? Let [Naaman] come now to me, that he may know that there is a prophet in Israel."...So Naaman came with his horses and chariots and stood at the door of Elisha's house. And Elisha sent a messenger to him, saying, "Go and wash in the Jordan seven times, and your flesh shall be restored, and you shall be clean." But Naaman was angry and went away, saying, "Behold, I thought that he would surely come out to me and stand and call upon the name of the LORD his God, and wave his hand over the place and cure the leper."...But his servants came near and said to him, "My father, it is a great word the prophet has spoken to you; will you not do it? Has he actually said to you, 'Wash, and be clean'?" So he went down and dipped himself seven times in the Jordan, according to the word of the man of God, and his flesh was restored like the flesh of a little child, and he was clean.

—2 KINGS 5:8–14

God moves in a mysterious way
His wonders to perform.

He plants His footsteps in the sea
and rides upon the storm.
                    —WILLIAM COWPER (1731–1800)

T HE KING OF Aram (Syria) writes a letter to the king
    of Israel, this letter probably being hand delivered by
    Naaman, the commander of the Syrian army, who
wants to be healed of his leprosy. The letter is met with
a violent reaction: "Am I God, to kill and to make alive,
that this man sends word to me to cure a man of his leprosy?" (v. 7). The letter to the king of Israel neglected to
mention a prophet.

What follows in this fascinating account are various
kinds of wisdom:

> And the king of Syria said [to Naaman], "Go now,
> and I will send a letter to the king of Israel."
>
> So he went, taking with him ten talents of silver,
> six thousand shekels of gold, and ten changes of
> clothing. And he brought the letter to the king of
> Israel, which read, "When this letter reaches you,
> know that I have sent to you Naaman my servant,
> that you may cure him of his leprosy." And when
> the king of Israel read the letter, he tore his clothes
> and said, "Am I God, to kill and to make alive, that
> this man sends word to me to cure a man of his
> leprosy? Only consider, and see how he is seeking a
> quarrel with me."
>
> But when Elisha the man of God heard that the
> king of Israel had torn his clothes, he sent to the
> king, saying, "Why have you torn your clothes? Let
> him come now to me, that he may know that there

is a prophet in Israel." So Naaman came with his horses and chariots and stood at the door of Elisha's house. And Elisha sent a messenger to him, saying, "Go and wash in the Jordan seven times, and your flesh shall be restored, and you shall be clean." But Naaman was angry and went away, saying, "Behold, I thought that he would surely come out to me and stand and call upon the name of the Lord his God, and wave his hand over the place and cure the leper. Are not Abana and Pharpar, the rivers of Damascus, better than all the waters of Israel? Could I not wash in them and be clean?" So he turned and went away in a rage. But his servants came near and said to him, "My father, it is a great word the prophet has spoken to you; will you not do it? Has he actually said to you, 'Wash, and be clean'?" So he went down and dipped himself seven times in the Jordan, according to the word of the man of God, and his flesh was restored like the flesh of a little child, and he was clean.

—2 KINGS 5:5–14

True wisdom has more than one definition, including this: knowing the next step forward in any situation. But not all wisdom is true wisdom. James 3:14–15 talks about wisdom that is not from above but below.

Why is this word important? First, true wisdom is the greatest possession on earth (Prov. 4:4–9). Second, this wisdom comes with a cost: "Though it cost you all you have," get it! (Prov. 4:7, NIV). The cost of wisdom often has to do with forfeiting your pride—for example, climbing down after you have lost your temper. This is what Naaman had to do before he was healed.

There is also *carnal* wisdom, which is based upon false assumptions. Naaman assumed he would have to buy his healing. This is why he brought money and gifts. This is typical of carnal wisdom—thinking that God operates as man does. In this world you get what you pay for. It is hard for some of us to make the transition from fleshly wisdom to true wisdom. However, Naaman was trapped by the way the king of Aram's letter was interpreted by the king of Israel. There was unfortunate wording, implying that the king of Israel would heal (v. 6). As I said, the king of Aram neglected to mention the prophet of Samaria, so the king of Israel panicked.

Naaman assumed he would meet the prophet. Being a general, he was used to great respect if not pomp and ceremony. But Elisha did not even invite him in or come out to meet him. Elisha sent a messenger to Naaman.

Over my twenty-five years at Westminster I would have some occasions to write a letter to Her Majesty the Queen. She always answered but never directly. Her secretary would say, "I am commanded by the Queen to thank you for your letter," or something similar. Elisha was not royal; he was a prophet of God, a man led by the Holy Spirit. He was not overly impressed by meeting a general. He did as he felt led; he sent a messenger

Carnal wisdom is displayed further by Naaman rejecting Elisha's response out of hand. Naaman went away angry. It is typical of carnal wisdom to lose your temper:

> This is not the wisdom that comes down from above, but is earthly, unspiritual, demonic.
>
> —James 3:15

Naaman assumed three things. First, he assumed he would meet Elisha. "I thought that he would surely come out to me." I was once invited to the White House, but I did not meet the president; I was among two hundred guests who heard him give a brief talk. Many people are invited to Number 10 Downing Street but don't meet the prime minister. Naaman assumed the prophet "would call upon the name of the Lord his God." At least he was right about that, but Elisha had already done that! Naaman thought Elisha would "wave his hand over the place" and cure his leprosy.

Carnal wisdom is not capable of thinking as God does. Naaman got two out of three right. But God said through Isaiah, "My ways are higher than your ways." (See Isaiah 55:9.) "There is a way that seems right to a man, but its end is the way to death" (Prov. 14:12).

Naaman's further carnal wisdom was demonstrated in his challenging Elisha's orders, namely, that he go dip in the Jordan River. Why the Jordan River? Naaman reasoned that the rivers in Damascus were better than any of the waters of Israel. This is fleshly type thinking. People also ask, Why go to church? Can't I pray at home? Why go to Toronto?

But in this story is also *concealed* wisdom. This is true wisdom but wisdom in which God's purpose is hidden. It sometimes seems strange. Elisha heard the news that the king tore his robes. But from what we learn of Elisha in all these stories, you can be sure he got the news from God directly. He then sent a message to the king at once (v. 8). Almost certainly the king already knew about Elisha's gift. In any case, the king told Naaman exactly where to go. People in high places should be informed where to go when they don't know for sure what to do when it comes to a man of God.

What Elisha ordered Naaman to do made no sense: "Go wash in the Jordan seven times, and your flesh shall be restored, and you shall be clean" (v. 10). There is no natural basis for water healing leprosy. Why the river of Jordan? Why seven times? What Elisha required was unspeakably humbling for the wealthy Syrian general. First, Elisha did not even come out to meet Naaman. Second, washing oneself in the Jordan was embarrassing. Having to do it seven times was all the more embarrassing.

Wisdom concealed is that for which there is no apparent hope or good reason. God told Abraham to sacrifice Isaac (Gen. 22:1–2). It made no sense. Mordecai the Jew refusing to bow to Haman seemed counterproductive (Est. 3:5). It made no sense. Jesus dying on a cross made no sense.

And yet in this story is also *challenged* wisdom. Elisha's order not only did not make sense to Naaman, but Naaman asked, "Are not Abana and Pharpar, the rivers of Damascus, better than all the waters of Israel?" The natural man always challenges God's wisdom. Likewise, we should expect those who hear our Gospel to challenge it.

There was, however, also *calming* wisdom. Elisha's word to the king had been calming; it diffused the king of Israel, and it encouraged both Naaman and the king of Israel that there was hope. The advice of Gamaliel to the Sanhedrin (Acts 5:38–39) was calming. The judge at Ephesus gave calming wisdom (Acts 19:38–41).

Finally, *convincing* wisdom is beautifully displayed when it comes from none other than Naaman's own servant. He said to Naaman: "My father, if the prophet had told you to do some great thing, would you not have done it? How much more, then, when he tells you, 'Wash and be cleansed'!" (v. 13, NIV). This was Naaman's servant speaking common sense to his master. One might ask, what might a great thing have been? Perhaps if Elisha had asked for a lot of money? Naaman would have given it. Or perhaps make Naaman do some great deed before people? Naaman would have done it. In other words, had Elisha asked something like this, Naaman would have no doubt obeyed Elisha. But Elisha asked a small thing. What is more, the prophet gave a promise: "He actually said to you, 'Wash, and be clean'?" (v. 13). The servant made sense to Naaman. He went against his carnal wisdom and obeyed the prophet Elisha:

> So he went down and dipped himself seven times in the Jordan, according to the word of the man of God, and his flesh was restored like the flesh of a little child, and he was clean (v. 14).

Jesus said he that is faithful in what is least will be faithful in much (Luke 16:10).

Calming wisdom led to convincing wisdom. Paul said to do the things that make for peace (Rom. 14:19). This is what the Gospel does: it leads to peace with God (Rom. 5:1) and to the peace of God (Phil. 4:7). Only the Holy Spirit can do the convincing when it comes to the Gospel. On the day of Pentecost, they were convinced when they asked, "What shall we do?" (Acts 2:37). Those who heard the word were baptized.

What Naaman conceded to do was not unlike a person being willing to be baptized; it was a humbling thing to do.

CHAPTER 12

SHEER GRATITUDE

Then [Naaman] returned to the man of God, he and all his company, and he came and stood before him [Elisha]. And he said, "Behold, I know that there is no God in all the earth but in Israel, so accept now a present from your servant." But he said, "As the LORD lives, before whom I stand, I will receive none." And he urged him to take it, but he refused. Then Naaman said, "If not, please let there be given to your servant two mule loads of earth, for from now on your servant will not offer burnt offering or sacrifice to any god but the LORD. In this matter may the LORD pardon your servant: when my master goes into the house of Rimmon, when I bow myself in the house of Rimmon, the LORD pardon your servant in this matter." He [Elisha] said to him, "Go in peace."

—2 KINGS 5:15–19

We need to discover all over again that worship is natural to the Christian, as it was to the godly Israelites who wrote the psalms, and that the habit of celebrating the greatness and graciousness of God yields an endless flow of thankfulness, joy, and zeal.

—J. I. PACKER (1926–2020)

Thankful people live longer.

—Mayo Clinic

Showing gratitude to God is the mark of a changed life. "Now I know that there is no God in all the world except in Israel" was the spontaneous comment of Naaman to Elisha after he saw the miracle of his healing from leprosy.

This chapter demonstrates the importance of gratitude. It is also a reminder of the wonderful benefit of "climbing down" when you realize you were wrong. This is what Naaman did—and got healed. It shows the kindness of God—that He heals people who are in pain. It also demonstrates the sovereignty of God.

Jesus referred to the healing of Naaman (Luke 4:27). This healing demonstrates God's love for people outside Israel and, as I said, His sovereignty, as in the words: "I will have mercy on whom I will have mercy, and I will have compassion on whom I will have compassion" (Rom. 9:15, NIV).

You will recall that Elisha was unimpressed with the entourage of Naaman; he only sent a message to him rather than invite him in or come out to meet him. Naaman, having started to leave in a rage, decided to listen to his servant and ended up doing what Elisha ordered: he dipped himself seven times in the river Jordan and was miraculously healed.

Climbing down is not an easy thing to do; it takes courage to swallow your pride.

Do you need to climb down? Have you dug in your

heels on a matter and said, "I will never admit I was wrong" or "I will never forgive them for what they did"?

There are some things to be seen in this chapter regarding the character and attributes of God. We live in the "me" generation; we ask, "What's in it for me?" I want us to focus on the God of the Bible and ask, "What's in it for God?"

THE SOVEREIGN WILL OF GOD

One of the missing and most needed notes today is the sovereignty of God. I define the sovereignty of God like this: God's right and power to do what He wants to do with anyone.

> In him we were also chosen, having been predestined according to the plan of him who works out everything in conformity with the purpose of his will.
> —EPHESIANS 1:11, NIV

> I will have mercy on whom I will have mercy, and I will have compassion on whom I will have compassion.
> —EXODUS 33:19; ROMANS 9:15, NIV

Jesus brought in the sovereignty of God at a surprising moment:

> There were many in Israel with leprosy in the time of Elisha the prophet, yet not one of them was cleansed—only Naaman the Syrian.
> —LUKE 4:27, NIV

This passage is a reminder from Jesus that God loves those outside Israel. It was foretelling God's love for Gentiles and that the healing of Naaman was by the sovereign will of God. Why Naaman? "I will have mercy on whom I will have mercy."

It is a reminder also that Naaman's healing and Elisha's gift are both demonstrations of the sovereignty of God. Gifts like this don't come along every day. The Samuels of this world are rare. The Elijahs of this world are rare. We should pray that God would raise up Elijahs and Elishas in our time!

Remember too that the same God who predestined the end also predestined the means. As for the amazing healing: Elisha ordered Naaman to dip seven times in Jordan. As for salvation, God has told us to preach the Gospel to every person (Mark 16:15).

SPONTANEOUS WORSHIP OF GOD

What follows is not forced but voluntary and spontaneous: "Now I know that there is no God in all the world except in Israel." That is what Naaman *chose* to say; it came freely and from his heart. It is the result of the sheer grace of God. The definition of the grace of God is *the unmerited favor flowing from the heart of God*.

God showed grace to Naaman. It meant that Naaman was a changed man—in more ways than one. Here is what we see in Naaman:

1. Repentance: Naaman "returned to the man of God" (v. 15). Repentance comes from the Greek *metanoia*: change of mind. It's a U-turn; climbing down. An essential part

of true conversion is repentance. The same
Naaman who left Elisha in a rage because
(1) Elisha did not come out to meet him
and (2) Elisha gave him the strange orders
to dip seven times in the Jordan changed
his tune.

2. Revelation: Naaman stood before Elisha and
said, "Now I know that there is no God in
all the world except in Israel" (v. 15, NIV).
This is an amazing revelation. Elisha did
not tell him to say that. It was certainly the
last thing Naaman expected; he was surprised. Dr. Martyn Lloyd-Jones often said
that a Christian is someone who is "surprised" that he or she is Christian.

Elisha agrees this time to meet Naaman. It is the first
time they have met. Naaman confesses to the truth of
God. There is no other God but this God. Jesus said, "I
am the way, and the truth, and the life. No one comes to
the Father except through me" (John 14:6). What Naaman
says is what the whole world will say one day: "At the
name of Jesus every knee should bow, in heaven and on
earth and under the earth, and every tongue confess that
Jesus Christ is Lord, to the glory of God the Father" (Phil.
2:10–11; see also Romans 14:11, NIV).

Naaman shows gratitude to God. This is why Naaman
went back—he wanted to thank Elisha. The essential
ingredient in sanctification is gratitude. Sanctification is
the doctrine of gratitude. We do not manifest holiness of

life to ensure we are saved. We do it to show gratitude to God. Sanctification: gratitude.

Thus, Naaman changes his tune, not only having climbed down from his rage but now wanting to show gratitude to Elisha. Unlike the nine that had been healed by Jesus (Luke 17:17), Naaman wants to show gratitude.

He meets Elisha and is profusely thankful. There are basically two kinds of gratitude: (1) spontaneous gratitude and (2) gratitude that must be taught. This is why the New Testament teaches gratitude.

> Do not be anxious about anything, but in every-
> thing by prayer and supplication with thanksgiving
> let your requests be made known to God.
> —Philippians 4:6

For most of us, we need to be taught.

In closing, let me revisit one of the most powerful experiences with God I ever had. After preaching on Philippians 4:6—just quoted—when I got to the phrase "with thanksgiving," my whole life came before me. I was stunned. Shocked. The Holy Spirit showed me countless moments when God had been so good to me, and I *did not thank Him*. I was so ashamed. After the sermon, I rushed to my desk in the vestry to pray, and I prayed like I never prayed in my life, with deepest repentance. I made a promise that day that for the rest of my life I would be a thankful man. That was thirty-five years ago. I will share with you something I have done every day since that Sunday morning I preached the sermon on Philippians 4:6. I go through my journal every morning and then thank God for every good thing that happened the day before. It is usually three or four things. I have never been the same since I began that.

I make a suggestion to you: think of at least three things every day to thank Him for. Do it before you go to bed each night. And if you need a little further coaxing, Mayo Clinic discovered that thankful people live longer.

CHAPTER 13

THE HONOR OF GOD

And when [Gehazi] came to the hill, he took [the two talents of silver] from their hand and put them in the house, and he sent the men away, and they departed. He went in and stood before his master, and Elisha said to him, "Where have you been, Gehazi?" And he said, "Your servant went nowhere." But he said to him, "Did not my heart go when the man turned from his chariot to meet you? Was it a time to accept money and garments, olive orchards and vineyards, sheep and oxen, male servants and female servants? Therefore the leprosy of Naaman shall cling to you and to your descendants forever." So he went out from his presence a leper, like snow.

—2 KINGS 5:24–27

I hold it to be a fact, that if all persons knew what each said of the other, there would not be four friends in the world.

—BLAISE PASCAL (1623–1662)

JONATHAN EDWARDS TAUGHT us that the one thing Satan cannot produce in us is a love for the glory of God. There are four noteworthy matters in this section of 2 Kings 5: (1) Elisha's refusal to accept a gift from Naaman,

(2) Naaman's request to take Israel's soil to Syria on which to kneel, (3) Naaman's request to go with the king of Syria into the temple of Rimmon, and (4) the judgment upon Gehazi for going behind Elisha's back to get some gifts from Naaman.

Let's look at the full passage:

> Then [Naaman] returned to the man of God, he and all his company, and he came and stood before him. And he said, "Behold, I know that there is no God in all the earth but in Israel; so accept now a present from your servant." But [Elisha] said, "As the LORD lives, before whom I stand, I will receive none." And he urged him to take it, but he refused. Then Naaman said, "If not, please let there be given to your servant two mule loads of earth, for from now on your servant will not offer burnt offering or sacrifice to any god but the LORD. In this matter may the LORD pardon your servant: when my master goes into the house of Rimmon to worship there, leaning on my arm, and I bow myself in the house of Rimmon, when I bow myself in the house of Rimmon, the LORD pardon your servant in this matter." But when Naaman had gone from him a short distance, Gehazi, the servant of Elisha the man of God, said [to himself], "See, my master has spared this Naaman the Syrian, in not accepting from his hand what he brought. As the LORD lives, I will run after him and get something from him." So Gehazi followed Naaman. And when Naaman saw someone running after him, he got down from the chariot to meet him and said, "Is all well?" And he said, "All is well. My master has sent me to say, 'There have just now come to me from the hill

country of Ephraim two young men of the sons of the prophets. Please give them a talent of silver and two changes of clothing.'" And Naaman said, "Be pleased to accept two talents." And he urged him and tied up two talents of silver in two bags, with two changes of clothing, and laid them on two of his servants. And they carried them before Gehazi. And when he came to the hill, he took them from their hand and put them in the house, and he sent the men away, and they departed. He went in and stood before his master, and Elisha said to him, "Where have you been, Gehazi?" And he said, "Your servant went nowhere." But he said to him, "Did not my heart go when the man turned from his chariot to meet you? Was it a time to accept money and garments, olive orchards and vineyards, sheep and oxen, male servants and female servants? Therefore the leprosy of Naaman shall cling to you and to your descendants forever." So he went out from his presence a leper, like snow.

—2 KINGS 5:15–27

This chapter is mostly about the honor of the true God. It shows the marks of a true servant of God, how a new convert wants to show honor to God. It demonstrates the somewhat surprising reasonableness of Elisha when Naaman wants Elisha's blessing on his having to accompany the crippled king of Syria into the temple of Rimmon. It shows that God is no respecter of persons; what Gehazi did, though the servant of the great prophet Elisha, must be judged.

THE REPUTATION OF GOD

Why did Elisha refuse a gift from Naaman? After all, Elisha had his own personal needs. Almost certainly he lived by financial support from those who believed him. But Elisha even swore an oath that he would not accept money from the grateful Naaman, still knowing Naaman only wanted to show gratitude.

Why then did Elisha refuse Naaman's gift? The answer is, first, Elisha knew that how he responded would be told far and wide. Elisha cared more about God's reputation in Syria than his own personal financial needs. You may recall that Paul would "rather die" than accept money from the Corinthians, although stating that a workman is worthy of his hire (1 Cor. 9:12). Abraham would not accept money from the king of Sodom lest he say, "I made Abraham rich" (Gen. 14:23). Abraham was thinking of God's reputation. Elisha wanted to make sure Naaman never forgot that God's mercy in healing him was without money! You cannot bribe the God of the Bible. It is also important to remember that Elisha even swore an oath— something that Naaman completely (wittingly or unwittingly) overlooked.

Naaman had made two requests to Elisha: (1) to take Israeli soil to Syria so he would be worshipping the God of Israel on Israeli soil and (2) to get Elisha's approval and thus be allowed to accompany the king of Syria when the handicapped king worshipped in the temple of Rimmon. Naaman would no more offer sacrifices to Rimmon, the god of Syria. He was truly a converted man! However, he was still under the king of Syria. Naaman anticipated a conflict down the road. He knew that when the aged and disabled king of Syria worshipped in the temple, he (Naaman) must be in attendance; he must help the king when the king bowed to a false god.

Elisha sets Naaman free: "Go in peace" (v. 19). Elisha does not say, "Shame on you, Naaman; it shows you have not been converted"—although some commentators do not excuse Elisha for this response. Elisha is not approving of anyone worshipping Rimmon—not at all. He is setting Naaman free to do what appears necessary for him. It is like attending a wedding in a church or place you would not personally approve of; we can be gracious without approving of the religion of the person getting married.

THE RETRIBUTION OF GOD

Jealousy, as well as greed and lying, got into Gehazi, the servant of Elisha, who was astonishingly disloyal. He showed a huge lack of respect for Elisha, not to mention Elisha's godly testimony and refusing money from Naaman on oath. This was a grievous sin. It shows how a person can be very close to a godly prophet and yet not be loyal to or affected by him. Gehazi had seen all the gold and silver and clothes that Naaman had brought to give Elisha a gift, but which Elisha refused. This infuriated Gehazi; he could not bear to see all that money get away from them when Elisha had been so gracious to Naaman.

Except for one thing: Gehazi was going to keep the money for himself—and not tell Elisha (so foolish of him). So he ran after Naaman before he got too far. It turns out that Gehazi also had servants. These servants would have been the responsibility of Elisha, which shows how Elisha could certainly have used the money Naaman offered.

Jealousy and greed set in. This too often happens in Christian work. It happened to Ananias and Sapphira: jealousy, greed, lying. And they wanted to be "very in" with those in the inner circle of the early church. Gehazi angrily vowed (swore an oath, "As surely as the Lord lives," v. 20) to get something from the wealthy Syrian general Naaman. What a dangerous thing to do! But Gehazi saw a way of getting some of it without Naaman suspecting what Gehazi was up to. He foolishly thought Elisha would not find out.

Gehazi almost succeeded! He got what he wanted—twice as much—from Naaman. He kept his venture secret—as if he could hide something like this from a prophet like Elisha. How foolish! Elisha asked Gehazi where he had been. Gehazi lied (v. 25). Ananias and Sapphira lied to the Holy Spirit. Gehazi lied to Elisha—perhaps tantamount to lying to the Holy Spirit, especially after seeing the glory of God in the incredible miracle.

What to me, however, is the most honorable thing about Elisha—not only in this account but in all his miracles combined—is this: Elisha made no attempt to get Naaman to see that Gehazi was doing this on his own. If I had been Elisha (this is what I would fear about myself) I would have made Gehazi go back to Naaman and confess that this was not Elisha's wish at all. But Elisha does not lift a finger to clear his name! That to me is incredible. Elisha appears willing to let Naaman think that Elisha really did ask for money after all. This to me shows what a godly man Elisha was. It demonstrates the truth: *let God do the vindicating, and let people think the worst of us unless God shows them different.*

Gehazi's punishment was terminal chastening. Whom

the Lord loves He chastens, or disciplines. Chastening is for the Christian, not the lost (Heb. 12:6–11). However, there are three kinds of chastening:

1. Internal (plan A)—through the Word by the Holy Spirit

2. External (plan B)—God dealing from without, such as sickness, loss of job, financial reverse, withholding of vindication

3. Terminal (plan C)—of which there are two kinds:
    a. Death (1 John 5:16; 1 Cor. 11:30)
    b. Permanent punishment in this life (Heb. 6:4–6)

Gehazi's punishment was not sudden death, as in the case of Ananias and Sapphira or like some Christians in the church (1 Cor. 11:30). It would be in a sense worse: he would live with leprosy the rest of his life.

It is interesting how Elisha questioned Gehazi. He knew what had happened, but he calmly put questions to him: "Where have you been?" (v. 25). This gave Gehazi a moment to repent and confess his sin then and there. But no. He lied and things went from bad to worse.

Whom the Lord loves He disciplines. Internal chastening is the best way for God to deal with your problem. Reading these very lines is God's plan A. God only turns to plan B when plan A doesn't work.

CHAPTER 14

A STRANGE MIRACLE

Now the sons of the prophets said to Elisha, "See, the place where we dwell under your charge is too small for us. Let us go to the Jordan and each of us get there a log, and let us make a place for us to dwell there." And he answered, "Go." Then one of them said, "Be pleased to go with your servants." And he answered, "I will go." So he went with them. And when they came to the Jordan, they cut down trees. But as one was felling a log, his axe head fell into the water, and he cried out, "Alas, my master! It was borrowed." Then the man of God said, "Where did it fall?" When he showed him the place, he cut off a stick and threw it in there and made the iron float. And he said, "Take it up." So he reached out his hand and took it.

—2 KINGS 6:1–7

Kindness is the language which the deaf can hear and the blind can see.

—MARK TWAIN (1835–1910)

ONLY GOD CAN turn water into wine. In this passage we see the strangest if not funniest of all the miracles of Elisha: an ax-head floating in the Jordan River. Compared to the healing of Naaman from leprosy, this is almost comical, ridiculous. This miracle does not make people well. It does not help anyone's finances.

Why would God do this? We must remember that God is the explanation of what Elisha does in this story. It is not what Elisha does, although it seems like that. It is what God does.

Why would God make an ax-head float?

Answer: God cares about every aspect of our lives. "In all your ways acknowledge him, and he will make straight your paths" (Prov. 3:6).

What grips me most about this story is not only the miracle but Elisha's availability, flexibility, and kindness. Elisha was an important man. He was famous in his day. He performed miracles that defy one's imagination. I have known some important people. But when I think of Elisha's role in this story, I am reminded of how some people are—or at least give the impression that they are—too lofty to be bothered with small things.

The sons of the prophets make two suggestions to Elisha: (1) Could we move elsewhere? Elisha says yes. (2) Will you go with us? Yes. Then comes the accident of a man's ax-head falling into the water, and Elisha gets it back for the man.

When that man lost the ax-head, it was a horrible moment for him—"it was borrowed."

Had it not been borrowed he possibly might not have thought twice about it. It meant more to this man to retrieve it than if it had been his own.

This miracle, by the way, is the type of miracle that cynics—especially those who don't believe in miracles—would seize upon to make Elisha look ridiculous. Imagine today a group of Charismatics or Pentecostals reporting that a piece of iron floated on the river Thames in London or the Cumberland River in Nashville. A good way to know? Consider how some talk about the Toronto Blessing or the reports of gold teeth in some places. (Regarding the gold teeth, I saw this once for myself. A ten-year-old Mexican girl screamed during a worship service and asked people to look inside her mouth. I looked in and saw gold teeth— where wisdom teeth are—with perfect symmetry. As tears ran down her cheeks, she kept crying out, "Why me?"). God loves to choose what some are likely to call foolish or silly. Yes. He chooses the foolish things of the world to confound the wise (1 Cor. 1:27). I sometimes reckon that the Father, Son, and Holy Spirit have a council and ask, "What is the next thing we can do to make people sneer or dismiss what We do?"

The Bible reports the floating of the ax-head as a fact, but it would be the perfect sort of miracle that cessationists and liberals would dismiss—or laugh at.

A miracle could be defined as an extraordinary event that blesses people but is beyond what is natural or explained scientifically. A "miracle drug" will have a scientific explanation; a miracle such as gold teeth being created in someone's jaw does not.

There are probably at least three levels of miracles: (1) creative miracles—such as new eyes, a stretched arm, not to mention someone being raised from the dead. It is my opinion that last-day miracles accompanying the second coming will bring these; (2) the healing of a headache or feeling of being unwell. Sometimes God steps in on things like this; (3) natural or scientifically originated miracles. These do have a natural explanation. Penicillin is an example. It is what scientists do. God, by common grace, or "special grace in nature," as John Calvin put it, is the explanation for good medicine. We still give the glory to God.

It is hard to categorize this ax-head floating miracle. No one's health is at stake; no one's financial security is at stake; no one's reputation is at stake. Only the embarrassed man who fears facing the owner of the ax-head to say, "Sorry, but I lost your ax-head."

However, the point is *God cared about that.*

THE STRATEGIC MAN OF GOD

Imagine having Elisha around! People like him don't show up every day. There had once been a Samuel, but no successor. Elijah showed up out of the blue, but Elisha was his successor. There was no successor to Elisha.

Those described in Hebrews 11 were strategic people. I would define a strategic person as a "sovereign vessel," one raised up by God with a specific ministry. He or she will be known for their gifting, courage, love, and influence for God. Amos talked about a "famine of hearing the word of the Lord" (Amos 8:11). What could be worse? Are we not close to such an era now?

But these men had Elisha around! They respected his authority; they wanted his approval. He respected their wish that he be with them. They would not always have Elisha. If you can get next to a true man of God, and he is willing to spend time with you, take this with all your strength and mind.

"I will," Elisha said when they asked him to be near

them. For my first four years at Westminster Chapel, I had Martyn Lloyd-Jones weekly and as often as I needed him. I cherish those days.

THE SECRET MYSTERY OF GOD

Accidents are going to happen. The question is: Does God cause them? Or does He merely "permit" them? I answer this way: the difference between what God causes and what God allows is holy ground. Take off your shoes. That is what God was teaching Moses at the burning bush. Don't try to figure it out!

Why did this son of a prophet, sitting at the feet of Elisha, lose his friend's ax-head? It fell into the Jordan River. They were cutting trees; this one was obviously near the riverbank. Elisha was around. What if he had not been around? Would the man have walked into the water to search? What we do know: the loss of the ax-head gave this man extreme anxiety. "It was borrowed."

God uses extreme anxiety to get our attention. The first reference to tears in the Bible is when Hezekiah wept because he was told he would die shortly (2 Kings 20:5). Tears got God's attention, and Hezekiah lived another fifteen years. In 2 Corinthians 1 Paul describes his greatest trial. It came, he said, that he might rely not on himself but on God (2 Cor. 1:9). The lost ax-head brought fear of great embarrassment; the man feared the embarrassment of having to explain to the owner. God knows we don't like to be embarrassed.

This story removes the superstitious notion that if you have an Elisha around you will have no unwanted occurrences. Billy Graham said that President Lyndon Johnson wanted a clergyman around when he had major crises.

Could the ax-head incident have been an attack of the devil? Billy Graham told me that at the beginning of every crusade they ever had, a satanic attack came. So was the ax-head falling into the river an attack of the devil? Perhaps. This was a time when Elisha was teaching prophets.

THE STRANGE MIRACLE OF GOD

When the man said, "Oh my lord…it was borrowed," it suggests that he was hoping Elisha would step in and find the ax-head. Elisha might have said to him, "Go into the water and find it yourself, you dummy!" The water was not all that deep; they would have waded around, the iron would have gone straight to the bottom, one could shuffle around with his feet and find it.

Elisha decided to get involved. "Where did it fall?" he asked. Why was this question necessary? This is where the miracle promises to be strange. Why is knowing where it fell and Elisha cutting a stick and throwing it in the water important? It is a mystery why Elisha did it this way. There is no rhyme or reason why Elisha would cut a stick and throw it where the iron ax-head went down. There is no rhyme or reason why Jesus spit into a blind man's eyes before He healed him (Mark 8:23). All we know: the man was healed. Likewise, all we know in this case: Elisha "made the iron float." He said, "Take it up." The man did, and the crisis was over. It saved the man embarrassment;

he would never have to tell the owner of the ax-head what had happened.

Another question we ask is this: Why did this man—one of the one hundred of the sons of the prophets—not do the miracle himself? Were they not there to learn from the great Elisha? Whatever was he teaching them? Why did this man not learn from Elisha? What was the "company of prophets" there for?

Charles Spurgeon said concerning his School of the Prophets: you cannot teach a person how to preach but you can teach him what to preach. But what was Elisha teaching these men? It shows there are levels of anointing. Elisha may not have been able to transfer his anointing to these men, but they could still learn from him. This shows that people today can have a prophetic gift and not be an Elisha. It shows that the gift of prophecy with ordinary people may not turn you into an Elisha.

We are all interested in miracles. Who wouldn't be? We surely want to see them. But I never forget those words of Carl F. H. Henry: "Only God can turn the water into wine."

Let's be careful with our language when we talk about a miracle. We may well be in the day of small things. Let us pray for the day of big things. A test could be that you and I are willing to accept a strange miracle—and let people laugh at us—if that is what God chooses to do.

CHAPTER 15

When God Is on Your Side

When the servant of the man of God rose early in the morning and went out, behold an army with horses and chariots was all around the city. And the servant said, "Alas, my master! What shall we do?" He said, "Do not be afraid, for those who are with us are more than those who are with them." Then Elisha prayed and said, "O Lord, please open his eyes that he may see." So the Lord opened the eyes of the young man, and he saw, and behold, the mountain was full of horses and chariots of fire all around Elisha.

—2 Kings 6:15–17

Helplessness is a place of power if you are helpless before God. Ask God for help in everything you do.

—Joyce Meyer

How do you know that God is for you—and not for your enemy?

At the height of the American Civil War in the 1860s, someone asked President Abraham Lincoln: "Is God on our side?" He replied: "I am more concerned that we are on the Lord's side."

> If the LORD had not been on our side…the flood
> would have engulfed us, the torrent would have
> swept over us, the raging waters would have swept
> us away.
>
> —PSALM 124:1, 4, NIV

> Then my enemies will turn back when I call for
> help. By this I will know that God is for me.
>
> —PSALM 56:9, NIV

In 1956 I was forced to make decisions that caused many in my family to doubt my wisdom. My grandpa McCurley spoke up in my behalf with these words: "I am for him right or wrong." Oh, how I needed to hear that!

The same king of Syria who had given Naaman permission to go to Israel to get healed of his leprosy is now at war with the king of Israel again. He makes plans to invade Israel. But something keeps going wrong; it seems as if one of his own has betrayed him; it looks like treachery (vv. 9–11). The culprit, however, is not one of Syria's own men who is telling things to the king of Israel. The culprit is none other than Elisha. They said to the king of Syria: "Elisha the prophet tells the king of Israel the very words you speak in your bedroom."

Let's look at the full passage together:

> Once when the king of Syria was warring against
> Israel, he took counsel with his servants, saying, "At
> such and such a place shall be my camp." But the
> man of God sent word to the king of Israel, "Beware
> that you do not pass this place, for the Syrians are
> going down there." And the king of Israel sent to
> the place about which the man of God told him.

Thus he was used to warn him, so that he saved himself there more than once or twice.

And the mind of the king of Syria was greatly troubled because of this thing, and he called his servants and said to them, "Will you not show me who of us is for the king of Israel?" And one of his servants said, "None, my lord, O king; but Elisha the prophet who is in Israel, tells the king of Israel the words you speak in your bedroom." And he said, "Go and see where he is, that I may send and seize him." It was told him, "Behold, he is in Dothan." So he sent there horses and chariots and a great army, and they came by night and surrounded the city.

When the servants of the man of God rose early in the morning and went out, behold an army with horses and chariots was all around the city. And the servant said, "Alas, my master! What shall we do?" He said, "Do not be afraid, for those who are with us are more than those who are with them." Then Elisha prayed and said, "O Lord, please open his eyes that he may see." So the Lord opened the eyes of the young man, and he saw, and behold, the mountain was full of horses and chariots of fire all around Elisha. And when the Syrians came down against him, Elisha prayed to the Lord and said, "Please strike this people with blindness." So he struck them with blindness in accordance with the prayer of Elisha. And Elisha said to them, "This is not the way, and this is not the city. Follow me, and I will bring you to the man whom you seek." And he led them to Samaria.

As soon as they entered Samaria, Elisha said, "O Lord, open the eyes of these men, that they may see." So the Lord opened their eyes and they saw, and behold, they were in the midst of Samaria. As soon as the king of Israel saw them, he said to Elisha, "My father, shall I strike them down? Shall I strike them down?" And he answered, "You shall not strike them down. Would you strike down those whom you have taken captive with your sword and with your bow? Set bread and water before them, that they may eat and drink and go to their master." So he prepared for them a great feast, and when they had eaten and drunk, he sent them away and they went to their master. And the Syrians did not come again on raids into the land of Israel.

—2 KINGS 6:8–23

The bottom line: the supreme God was on the side of Israel, not Aram (Syria). As Paul put it, "If God is for us, who can be against us?" (Rom. 8:31). The most important thing in the world is to know that God is on your side.

The question is: How can we know that God is on our side—and not on the side of our enemy?

PROPHETIC GIFT

Elisha, who had double the anointing of Elijah, happens to be on Israel's side. However, as Jesus said, there were many lepers in Israel, but only Naaman the Syrian was healed (Luke 4:27). We see this as an example of the sovereignty of God. God chose Israel.

How soon one forgets! The king of Syria is now going to war with the same king of Israel to whom he sent Naaman to be healed of leprosy. One would have thought this would diffuse hostile relationships. The heart is desperately wicked; who can know it? (Jer. 17:9). How fortunate Israel was to have Elisha the prophet.

What is the advantage of having a prophet like Elisha around? The answer: *God reveals the secrets and plans of the enemy.* The king of Syria decides to go to "this place." When they get there it is obvious that someone is working against them, as if their plans are revealed to Israel by a traitor. No; God is on Israel's side. Elisha knows the very words the king of Syria speaks in his bedroom—that is as private as one can get, but it is known to God. Nothing is hid from God: "Before there is a word on my tongue, you, Lord, know it completely" (Ps. 139:4, niv).

God is omniscient, all-knowing. He knows what we are thinking; He knows what our enemy is thinking. He knows who is faithful to Him and cannot be bribed. Elisha would not take any gift from Naaman. He let Syria know that God is a gracious God. Elisha did not try to protect his own reputation. He did not chase after Gehazi and say, "Don't let Naaman think I put you up to that lie." Elisha cared about one thing: what God thought of him.

PROPHETIC GUIDANCE

Elisha is governed by two things: what we might call *logos* and *rhema*. Although these two words can be used interchangeably, it is generally thought that prophetic words are *rhema* words but always cohere with the whole Word of God.

What God does next is almost always surprising and unpredictable.

The king of Aram decided to capture Elisha. But Elisha was warned of this too. You cannot fight against God!

The king of Syria sent horses and chariots at night. At dawn they surrounded the city. The new servant (successor to Gehazi) panicked when he saw the chariots surrounding the city of Dothan. Elisha did not panic: "Do not be afraid: those who are with us are more than those with them" (v. 16).

This is the key verse in this scenario. Elisha prayed for the servant to see what Elisha saw: "the hills full of horses and chariots of fire all around Elisha." (By the way, this is the source of the movie title *Chariots of Fire*.) The explanation: angels.

> The angel of the LORD encamps around those who
> fear him, and delivers them.
> —PSALM 34:7

> He will command his angels concerning you to
> guard you in all your ways.
> —PSALM 91:11

If all of us could see with our spiritual eyes (as Elisha did) we would see angels all around us here today. Elisha's prayer: "Strike these people with blindness" (v. 18). They were not totally blind, but they were kept from seeing exactly where they were. Elisha's plan was to get them to Samaria where they would not know where they were; they were led to Samaria without knowing it.

Elisha's second prayer was: now open their eyes so they can see where they are! Lo and behold, they were now inside Samaria. They were now vulnerable to Israel's king's command.

PROPHETIC GRACIOUSNESS

The enemy of Israel was now handed to the king of Israel on a silver platter. The king of Israel said to Elisha, "Shall I kill them? My father? Shall I kill them?" Here was the king's chance to say, "Gotcha"—and destroy them. Notice the change in the king's attitude toward Elisha. He had resented Elisha in the past. Now he calls him "my father."

Here was the opportunity for Israel to wipe out their enemy. But Elisha says, "Don't kill them. Treat them as you would have had you captured them" (v. 22). In other words, be gracious to them. Wine and dine them. Instead of playing "Gotcha," the king has a banquet for them!

This was an example of total forgiveness. Graciousness: when you could throw the book at them but let them off the hook instead. Never in the history of war had anything like this happened. Peace without shedding any blood! "And the Syrians did not come again on raids into the land of Israel" (v. 23).

It worked!

Who would have dreamed an outcome like this? The God of the Bible is a God of peace (1 Thess. 5:23). "I am for peace...they are for war" (Ps. 120:7).

Do you have an opportunity to let your enemy off the hook? Do you have "the goods" on them? Try something different: you forgive them. What an opportunity! Peace is better than war.

How to know God is for you and not your enemy? You cannot be bought off or bribed. You care about God's reputation, not your own. You show graciousness instead of getting even.

God will fight your battle.

CHAPTER 16

TRYING TO OUTGUESS GOD

But Elisha said, "Hear the word of the LORD: thus says the LORD, 'Tomorrow about this time a seah of fine flour shall be sold for a shekel, and two seahs of barley for a shekel, at the gate of Samaria.'" Then the captain on whose hand the king leaned said to the man of God, "If the LORD himself should make windows in heaven, could this thing be?" But he said, "You shall see it with your own eyes, but you shall not eat of it."…So a seah of fine flour was sold for a shekel, and two seahs of barley for a shekel, according to the word of the LORD. Now the king had appointed the captain on whose hand he leaned to have charge of the gate. And the people trampled him in the gate, so that he died, as the man of God had said when the king came down to him.

—2 KINGS 7:1–2, 16–17

God is predictably unpredictable.

—ANONYMOUS

O NE DAY GOD will clear His name, but how He will do this "no eye has seen nor ear heard nor has entered into the heart of man." What God has prepared for those who wait for Him (see Isaiah 64:4; 1 Corinthians 2:9), no one could predict. Which is more extraordinary: How God will clear His name on the day of judgment, or Elijah's prophecy being perfectly fulfilled?

This prophecy of Elisha is one of the most extraordinary, most complicated, and strangest of all his predictions in his ministry—if not the entire Old Testament. Consider how this chapter begins. No man could have made up this prophecy; neither could anybody on the planet have predicted how it could possibly come to pass. I doubt Elisha knew! It was shown to him and he obeyed, but I doubt he knew all that would bring the prophecy to pass. Maybe he did, maybe he didn't. But one thing is for sure: God knew. And God knows how He will clear His own name on the last day. He is the most hated person in the universe. People love Hitler more than they do the God of the Bible. How He will explain how a God of love, mercy, and power could allow suffering and evil as He has done, who knows? He knows.

In this chapter we will show how a prophecy is not only often misunderstood but fulfilled in a way that takes everybody by surprise.

> But Elisha said, "Hear the word of the LORD: thus says the LORD, 'Tomorrow about this time a seah of fine flour shall be sold for a shekel, and two seahs of barley for a shekel, at the gate of Samaria.'" Then the captain on whose hand the king leaned said to the man of God, "If the LORD himself should make windows in heaven, could this thing be?" But he said, "You shall see it with your own eyes, but you shall not eat of it."

Now there were four men who were lepers at the entrance to the gate. And they said to one another, "Why are we sitting here until we die? If we say, 'Let us enter the city,' the famine is in the city, and we shall die there. And if we sit here, we die also. So now come, let us go over to the camp of the Syrians. If they spare our lives we shall live, and if they kill us we shall but die." So they arose at twilight to go to the camp of the Syrians. But when they came to the edge of the camp of the Syrians, behold, there was no one there. For the Lord had made the army of the Syrians hear the sound of chariots and the horses, the sound of the great army, so they said to one another, "Behold, the king of Israel has hired against us the kings of the Hittites and the kings of Egypt to come against us." So they fled away in the twilight and abandoned their tents, their horses, and their donkeys, leaving the camp as it was, and fled for their lives. And when these lepers came to the edge of the camp, they went into a tent and ate and drank, and they carried off silver and gold and clothing and went and hid them. Then they came back and entered another tent and carried off things from it and went and hid them.

Then they said to one another, "We are not doing right. This is a day of good news. If we are silent and wait until the morning light, punishment will overtake us. Now therefore come; let us go and tell the king's household." So they came and called to the gatekeepers of the city and told them, "We came to the camp of the Syrians, and behold, there was no one to be seen or heard there, nothing but the horses tied and the donkeys tied and the tents as they were." Then the gatekeepers called out, and it was told within the king's household. And the king rose in the night and said to his servants, "I will tell you what the Syrians have done to us. They know that we are hungry. Therefore they have gone out of the camp to hide themselves in the open country, thinking, 'When they come out of the city, we shall take them alive and get into the city.'" And one of his servants said, "Let some men take five of the remaining horses, seeing that those who are left will fare like the whole multitude of Israel who have already perished. Let us send and see." So they took two horsemen, and the king sent them after the army of the Syrians, saying, "Go and see." So they went after them as far as the Jordan, and behold, all the way was littered with garments and equipment that the Syrians had thrown away in their haste. And the messengers returned and told the king.

Then the people went out and plundered the camp of the Syrians. So a seah of fine flour was sold for a shekel, and two seahs of barley for a shekel, according to the word of the LORD. Now the king had appointed the captain on whose hand he leaned to have charge of the gate. And the people trampled him in the gate, so that he died, as the man of God had said when the king came down to him. For when the man of God had said to the king, "Two seahs of barley shall be sold for a shekel, and a seah of fine flour for a shekel, about this time tomorrow in the gate of Samaria," the captain had answered the man of God, "If the LORD himself should make windows in heaven, could such a thing be?" And he said, "You shall see it with your own eyes, but you

shall not eat of it." And so it happened to him, for
the people trampled him in the gate and he died.

—2 Kings 7:1–20

The king of Aram (Syria) decided to attack Israel
again; he organized a siege in Samaria. A siege is "a military operation in which enemy forces surround a town
or building, cutting off essential supplies, with the aim
of compelling those inside to surrender."[1] There was an
extreme famine in the land. Strange as it seems, this is
the same king of Syria who sent Naaman to Israel to be
healed!

EXTREME FAMINE

The siege was working, one might say. Here is how bad it
was. It doesn't get much worse than this: a donkey's head
sold for eighty shekels of silver. A donkey's head would
not be taken as food except in extreme circumstances.
Pigeon dung was sold for five shekels. People were eating
their babies (2 Kings 6:25–29).

EVIL FURY

The king of Israel and many of the people were actually
blaming Elisha for all the pain and suffering. Wearing
sackcloth was a visible sign of mourning in those days.
The king was now wearing sackcloth. Filled with evil,
hate, and anger, he said: "May God do so to me and more
also, if the head of Elisha the son of Shaphat remains on
his shoulders today" (2 Kings 6:31). He was taking his
anger out on Elisha! Because Elisha had done such miracles in the past, the king was now angry that Elisha had
not come through for Israel again.

There are those today who claim that the real purpose in prayer is to change the will of God. Wrong! Our purpose in prayer is to discover what His will is—and obey it. Even Jesus did not try to change the Father's will. He only did what He saw the Father do (John 5:19). Elisha is, in a sense, a type of Christ. That means someone who makes you think of Jesus before Jesus came. Joseph was also a type of Christ (Gen. 37–50).

Elisha had done nothing wrong whatever. But people sometimes tend to blame not only God for negative things but the church as well! This also shows how terrible things can happen when a true man of God is still around. Never think that the presence of a Moses or Daniel or Paul will cause evil conditions to change.

The king of Israel swore an oath: Elisha will be beheaded by sundown. He was walking in the footsteps of Jezebel. She swore the same kind of oath regarding Elijah (1 Kings 19:2).

There are solemn warnings in the Old Testament: don't make a vow you can't keep. Both Jezebel and the king of Israel failed in this.

Elisha was one jump ahead of the king. Elisha was very much in the middle of all this—even if we have not heard from him. The king's official gets involved, saying, "This trouble is from the LORD! Why should I wait for the LORD any longer?" (2 Kings 6:32–33). The king is possibly using this as an excuse to kill Elisha since God has brought all this.

EXTRAORDINARY FORECAST

Elisha now involves himself in this extreme famine. When there is a major crisis and one does not hear from the Lord, mark it down: God is fully aware of all that is going on. God also has a plan. Elisha speaks and gives the extraordinary prophecy we have referred to about the price of flour and barley. He gives what appears to be an outlandish prophecy—the promise of prosperity and more than enough food. It is given to the king's messenger, but Elisha adds: you won't be around to enjoy it (2 Kings 7:2).

The prophecy indicated that there would not only be food but that it would be cheap, whereas at the moment food was extremely expensive. There would be six times as much good food for one-fifth of the price! It would be the equivalent of an abundance of food. But someone replied: even if it started raining with fierceness that prophecy could not be fulfilled.

This is why I compare the equivalent promise: that one day God will clear His name.

Some say, "God has a lot to answer for." Jesus declared: I am the Alpha and the Omega, the first and the last. God will have the last and final word.

> As I live, says the Lord, every knee shall bow to me, and every tongue shall confess to God.
>
> —ROMANS 14:11

> At present, we do not yet see everything in subjection to him. But we see him who for a little while was made lower than the angels, namely Jesus, crowned with glory and honor because of the

suffering of death, so that by the grace of God he
might taste death for everyone.
—HEBREWS 2:8–9

At the moment this doesn't seem likely or possible.

ELSEWHERE FACTOR

What I am calling the "elsewhere factor" is always opera-
tive and forgotten: what God is doing elsewhere in the
world. He is not focused on just you and me—where we
are—in Tennessee, London, or New York. He is focused
on Indonesia, China, the Philippines, the Middle East.
*What God is doing in places we don't think about will even-
tually be related directly to our situation here!*

So what we have in this story is a parallel situation.
Something is going on elsewhere: four Israelite lepers
escape to the Aramean/Syrian camp and find it deserted.
Who would have thought that four insignificant and
neglected lepers would figure into God's plan for Israel?
They eat Syrian food then feel guilty that they don't share
this with the king of Israel. "We are not doing what is
right," they say to each other. So they send word to the
king's palace; the king rejects the news but let's someone
test whether it is true. It turns out to be true, and they
bring a lot of food back. The place erupts; people are
starved; they run over each other, racing to get something
to eat.

EXACT FULFILLMENT

The messenger of the king is trampled and dies. He saw
the food, as Elisha prophesied, but he did not eat of it.
Food for everybody arrives. There is so much food that

the price goes way down: the prophecy is the exact fulfillment of what Elisha predicted (vv. 18–19). The food comes from the Aramean camp where the four lepers found it. The officer rejects the prophecy of Elisha. The king at first rejects the good news of the four lepers.

The truth is that Elisha did come through, giving an unlikely prophecy that was fulfilled and gave food in the time of famine.

How quickly people turn against God and His prophet. The most unlikely and outlandish prophecy was truly of God. Elisha had appeared unvindicated for a while. This story shows how God would clear Elisha's name. It shows how God can clear His own name—in a brief period of time.

The fulfillment of a prophecy is often not carried out in the way you would expect. No human being could have guessed or even come close to the way this prophecy was fulfilled.

God loves to do this. It is one of His ways.

CHAPTER 17

INSIDE INFORMATION

Now Elisha had said to the woman whose son he had restored to life, "Arise, and depart with your household, and sojourn wherever you can, for the LORD has called for a famine and it will come upon the land for seven years." So the woman arose and did according to the word of the man of God. She went with her household and sojourned in the land of the Philistines seven years. And at the end of the seven years, when the woman returned from the land of the Philistines, she went to appeal to the king for her house and her land. Now the king was talking with Gehazi the servant of the man of God, saying, "Tell me all the great things that Elisha has done." And while he was telling the king how Elisha had restored the dead to life, behold, the woman whose son he had restored to life appealed to the king for her house and her land. And Gehazi said, "My lord, O king, here is the woman, and here is her son whom Elisha restored to life." And when the king asked the woman, she told him. So the king appointed an official for her, saying, "Restore all that was hers, together with all the produce of the fields from the day that she left the land to now."

—2 KINGS 8:1–6

Information may inform the mind, but revelation
sets a heart on fire.

—MATT REDMAN

ONCE YOU BECOME a Christian, you are made a
member of a special family: God is your Father,
Jesus is your elder brother, and the Holy Spirit
is your guide.

It turns out that Elisha gave the wealthy Shunammite
woman inside information. The information was actually
revelation. It was information known only to God. But
the Holy Spirit was pleased to share some of this information with Elisha, and he felt led to share it with the
Shunammite woman, whose son he had raised from the
dead. He did this with regard to a natural crisis that
began seven years before. We learn that Elisha gave the
Shunammite woman a tip, so she acted on it and took her
family to the land of the Philistines for seven years.

Inside information is knowledge not generally available
to the public. It is information of a precise nature. When
it comes to the price of stocks, however, inside information is illegal. The use of inside information to protect the
price of shares publicly is a criminal offense.

The Shunammite woman was given some inside information: the Holy Spirit revealed a bit of God's will to her
regarding the next several years—a famine was coming.

EXCEPTIONAL PRIVILEGE

Not everybody has an Elisha for a friend. Elisha was in touch with the Most High God. He shared this with the Shunammite.

This is a reminder that Jesus had special friends. In John 11 we discover that He was close to Lazarus and his sisters, Mary and Martha. What a privilege to have a relationship with Jesus like that!

As for the Shunammite, we might ask: Had not God done enough for her already? She was wealthy—"well to do," as it is put in 2 Kings 4:8. Not only that, but God raised her son from the dead. We use the expression "enough is enough," but it usually refers to tragedy. Yet we might say this regarding the wealthy Shunammite: enough is enough. She is wealthy, has Elisha for a close friend, and has a son who was raised from the dead! Now she gets advance notice of a famine and is able to avoid it.

God's mercies are exhaustless. This is the way He is. He also decides on whom He will show mercy: "I will have mercy on whom I will have mercy" (Exod. 33:19; Rom. 9:15). This is what we mean by the sovereignty of God. Moreover, His mercies endure forever (Ps. 118:1, KJV).

Elisha told the Shunammite woman: "Go away with your family." This is a reminder that God wants families to stay together. Elisha was ensuring that the famine did not divide her family. In my book *In Pursuit of His Glory* (an account of my twenty-five years at Westminster Chapel) I confess that my greatest regret is that I did not put my family first in those years.

Elisha told the Shunammite, "Stay for a while." It would be a temporary exile from home. He also said,

"Stay wherever you can"—making no attempt to control her; he was setting her free to go where she chose. She was given special information—in this case, revelation. It would not be good to be given this special knowledge and not listen to Elisha.

Christians have access to inside information. For example, we have been warned of the coming wrath of God. (Matt. 3:7). We are told that the blood of Jesus satisfies the wrath and judgment of God (Rom. 5:9). We are also taught that Jesus will come and judge the earth (Matt. 24:44).

ETERNAL PURPOSE

There are some things we cannot change; God has decreed them. It turns out that God decreed that a famine lasting seven years (v. 1) would ravage the "land"—obviously it was for Israel only. The "land" meant Israel. God had a special love for Israel, and there was purpose in what He decreed. There was a set time for this famine: seven years. It is a reminder that every trial has a built-in time frame. God knows how long a trial will last. You and I may not know these times in advance.

We are also reminded that it is not a prophet's prerogative to change God's will; it is his responsibility to reveal God's will. Even Elisha could not change this; all he could do was reveal God's will.

This also shows that God knows the future. But this warning was given only to the Shunammite woman as far as we know. Apparently Elisha was not allowed to tell all Israel.

Does it surprise you that God controls the weather? Does it surprise you that God can bring disaster? Some say the COVID pandemic was from the devil since God would not cause bad things. Really? God brings both. This is a clear teaching throughout the Bible.

Elijah, Elisha's mentor, was given such authority that it would not rain unless he said so (1 Kings 17:1).

EXTRAORDINARY PROVIDENCE

The Shunammite stayed in the land of the Philistines for seven years—in enemy territory! This area was fertile, good for growing vegetation, and was not affected by the famine.

Are you in exile? Living in enemy territory? Why? Perhaps it is to make you appreciate what you have at home—to see how the rest of the world lives and make you more thankful. David lived in exile; he waited for God to return him to Jerusalem.

At the end of seven years the Shunammite lady returns, only to find her home and land in the hands of dishonest and unscrupulous neighbors. She is distraught but does not go to Elisha, nor blame him. She goes through proper channels—to the king. She goes to the king to "beg," asking for mercy. There is no feeling of entitlement!

Meanwhile Gehazi, now a leper (owing to Elisha's pronouncement of judgment on him) is with the king. While Gehazi is with the king, the king asks to hear some "Elisha stories." (I have Martyn Lloyd-Jones stories, Paul Cain stories, Arthur Blessitt stories.)

We can eavesdrop and guess what Gehazi tells the king:

- "Death in the pot"

- axe handle floating

- the healing of Naaman—and how Gehazi was made a leper

- prophecy of Elisha promising food when all was bleak

- the Shunammite's child being raised from the dead

At that very moment the Shunammite comes to the king with her plea. But Gehazi exclaims, "This is the same woman I have been telling you about!" There is more: "Here is her son too"—possibly a teenager now. The king turns to the woman: "Is this really true?" It is a most amazing providence.

EXTRAORDINARY PROVISION

The king assigned an official to her case, saying to him: "Give back everything that belonged to her, including all the income from her land from the day she left the country until now" (v. 6). When the king said, "Give back everything that belonged to her," he was not only respecting the woman but Elisha!

Think of this: give her back everything including the income she would have received. It is breathtaking goodness from God. But it is, as Paul said, God giving us beyond all we could ask or think (Eph. 3:20).

All this was the culmination of two things: (1) inside information, or revelation, and (2) an amazing providence. Some would call it "coincidence" that Gehazi was telling Elisha stories to the king at the precise moment the Shunammite showed up. It goes to show: God is never too late, never too early, but always just on time. By being a part of the Shunammite's life, the king had the privilege of being right in the middle of what God was doing. Moreover, this was the king who had been ruthless toward Elisha at one time.

Is it fair that the Christian has insider information? You can have this too! The Christian is a part of a special family; we do have a special advantage: (1) God forgives us all our sins, (2) supplies all our need, (3) shapes our past (Rom. 8:28), (4) gives inside information not available to those outside the family, and (5) gives you a home in Heaven when you die.

This family is different from other families. With other families, you must be born into it. Some are born to privilege. All in the family of God are born to privilege; we have been born-again—we are all royal. You can be a part of the Christian family by accepting the open invitation to come in.

Are you outside the family? *Come on in!* The only qualification (and it is not being well-connected, brilliant, clever, or educated) is being aware of your need of Him, aware that you are thirsty. If you are thirsty, come and drink. Whosoever will, let him drink (Rev. 22:17)!

CHAPTER 18

A Prophet's Pain

And the man of God wept. And Hazael said, "Why does my lord weep?" He answered, "Because I know the evil that you will do to the people of Israel. You will set on fire their fortresses, and you will kill their young men with the sword and dash in pieces their little ones and rip open their pregnant women." And Hazael said, "What is your servant, who is but a dog, that he should do this great thing?" Elisha answered, "The Lord has shown me that you are going to be king over Syria." Then he departed from Elisha and came to his master, who said to him, "What did Elisha say to you?" And he answered, "He told me that you would certainly recover." But the next day he took the bed cloth and dipped it in water and spread it over his face, till he died. And Hazael became king in his place.

—2 Kings 8:11–15

The pain I feel now is the happiness I had before. That's the deal.

—C. S. Lewis (1898–1963)

D O YOU WANT a double anointing? Are you sure? It is what Elisha wanted so earnestly—and got it. But we now look further at the pain of a prophet. The greater the anointing, the greater the suffering.

The pain of a prophet consists of many things. Being misunderstood. Having people blame you when their anger is toward God. Having people pester you for "a word." That is what begins this section. The king of Syria was ill and wanted a word from Elisha. But in this chapter, we see more pain still that a prophet experiences. He sees dreadful, horrible, and painful things that lie in the future. Elisha weeps because he sees what is coming down the road: that the enemy will do unthinkably evil things. It is part of the deal. When Elijah's mantle fell on Elisha it no doubt made him a very, very happy man. But part of the double anointing package is to see pain and suffering other people do not see.

The full passage reads:

> Now Elisha came to Damascus. Ben-hadad the king of Syria was sick. And when it was told him, "The man of God has come here," the king said to Hazael, "Take a present with you and go to meet the man of God, and inquire of the LORD through him, saying, 'Shall I recover from this sickness?'" So Hazael went to meet him, and took a present with him, all kinds of goods of Damascus, forty camels' loads. When he came and stood before him, he said, "Your son Ben-hadad king of Syria has sent me to you, saying, 'Shall I recover from this sickness?'" And Elisha said to him, "Go, say to him, 'You shall certainly recover,' but the LORD has shown me that

he shall certainly die." And he fixed his gaze and stared at him, until he was embarrassed.

And the man of God wept. And Hazael said, "Why does my lord weep?" He answered, "Because I know the evil that you will do to the people of Israel. You will set on fire their fortresses, and you will kill their young men with the sword and dash in pieces their little ones and rip open their pregnant women." And Hazael said, "What is your servant, who is but a dog, that he should do this great thing?" Elisha answered, "The LORD has shown me that you are going to be king over Syria." Then he departed from Elisha and came to his master, who said to him, "What did Elisha say to you?" And he answered, "He told me that you would certainly recover." But the next day he took the bed cloth and dipped it in water and spread it over his face, till he died. And Hazael became king in his place.

—2 KINGS 8:7–15

Does it surprise you that Elisha would say to Hazael, the next king of Syria, "Tell King Ben-Hadad he will live but he will in fact die"? Is Elisha guilty of telling a lie? Is the man of God sinning by telling Hazael to lie? What business is it of Elisha's to be giving prophetic words to the enemy of Israel?

When Elisha said to Hazael that the king of Syria would die, Elisha stared at the very man he knew would kill him. And Elisha wept. The pain was awful for the prophet. Hazael lost no time to murder Ben-Hadad to become the next king. Elisha saw it coming.

I would say to you, dear reader, should you be among those who think they want a double anointing, think again! It is not all glamour and having people stand in awe of you.

A lawyer came to me in the vestry at Westminster Chapel to say, "I believe I am called to preach." I said, "I suggest you test it by joining us on the streets this Saturday when we talk to passersby about Jesus." He replied: "I am not good at talking to one person, but I can speak ably to thousands." He was not happy with my suggestion. He saw being in the pulpit as a place of glamour and being admired. This is why Charles Spurgeon warned people, "Be sure you are called before you say you want to be a preacher. *If you can do anything else, do it.*"

Why would Elisha go to Damascus? He possibly did not know why himself until he got there. He found out. God let Elisha in on painful secrets that pertained to Israel.

We live in a wicked world. It is not getting better and better but worse and worse. Paul said that in the last days, "Evil people and impostors will go from bad to worse" (2 Tim. 3:13).

Do not believe the nonsense propagated by some today who want you to believe things in the world are getting better and better. They are not.

CHAPTER 19

OBEDIENCE IN
SMALL THINGS

Then Elisha the prophet called one of the sons of
the prophets and said to him, "Tie up your garments, and take this flask of oil and go to Ramoth-
gilead. And when you arrive, look there for Jehu the
son of Jehoshaphat, son of Nimshi. And go in and
have him rise from among his fellows, and lead him
to an inner chamber. Then take the flask of oil and
pour it on his head and say, 'Thus says the LORD,
I anoint you king over Israel.' Then open the door
and flee: do not linger."

—2 KINGS 9:1–3

There are many of us that are willing to do great
things for the Lord, but few of us are willing to do
the small things.

—DWIGHT L. MOODY (1837–1899)

ELISHA IS GETTING older and decides to ask one of
the one hundred sons of the prophets to do what
he himself would normally do. This is the first hint
that Elisha—the successor to Elijah, who did not die but
was transported to Heaven—might die a natural death.
We have no way of knowing whether Elisha was secretly

hoping that his double anointing might include being taken to Heaven as Elijah was. Maybe yes, maybe no.

We have wondered whatever would happen to those one hundred sons of the prophets. This is the first hint that God would use them. Elisha picks one of them to stand in for him.

What an honor to do so.

> Then Elisha the prophet called one of the sons of the prophets and said to him, "Tie up your garments, and take this flask of oil and go to Ramoth-gilead. And when you arrive, look there for Jehu the son of Jehoshaphat, son of Nimshi. And go in and have him rise from among his fellows, and lead him to an inner chamber. Then take the flask of oil and pour it on his head and say, 'Thus says the LORD, I anoint you king over Israel.' Then open the door and flee: do not linger." So the young man, the servant of the prophet, went to Ramoth-gilead. And when he came, behold, the commanders of the army were in council. And he said, "I have a word for you, O commander." And Jehu said, "To which of us all?" And he said, "To you, O commander." So he arose and went into the house. And the young man poured the oil on his head, saying to him, "Thus says the LORD, the God of Israel, I anoint you king over the people of the LORD, over Israel. And you shall strike down the house of Ahab your master, so that I may avenge on Jezebel the blood of my servants the prophets, and the blood of all the servants of the LORD. For the whole house of Ahab shall perish, and I will cut off from Ahab every male, bond or free, in Israel. And I will make

the house of Ahab like the house of Jereboam the son of Nebat, and like the house of Baasha the son of Ahijah. And the dogs shall eat Jezebel in the territory of Jezreel, and none shall bury her." Then he opened the door and fled. When Jehu came out to the servants of his master, they said to him, "Is all well? Why did this mad fellow come to you?" And he said to them, "You know the fellow and his talk." And they said, "That is not true; tell us now." And he said, "Thus and so he spoke to me, saying, 'Thus says the LORD, I anoint you king over Israel.'" Then in haste every man of them took his garment and put it under him on the bare steps and they blew the trumpet and proclaimed, "Jehu is king."

—2 KINGS 9:1–13

I once stood in for Dr. Martyn Lloyd-Jones, preaching for him in Bedford, England. No one announced that he would not be there. I dreaded facing the people who wanted to hear him. But it was an honor nonetheless that the doctor asked me to take his place.

We may ask: What if that one chosen to anoint Jehu never did anything again—for Elisha or in any other capacity? Answer: *it was an honor to do it once*! He would talk about this for the rest of his life—telling his children and grandchildren: "I once took Elisha's place."

Jesus said that he who is faithful in what is least is the one who will be faithful in much (Luke 16:10). It is a high honor to do *anything* the Lord tells us to do. And don't forget: this unknown servant of Elisha was anointing an Israelite king—no small matter. As we used to sing, "Little is much when God is in it"!

CHAPTER 20

A Prophet's Legacy

So Elisha died, and they buried him. Now bands of
Moabites used to invade the land in the spring of
the year. And as a man was being buried, behold, a
marauding band was seen and the man was thrown
into the grave of Elisha, and as soon as the man
touched the bones of Elisha, he revived and stood
on his feet.

—2 Kings 13:14–21

I have talked with great men, and I do not see how
they differ from others.

—Abraham Lincoln (1809–1865)

E LISHA APPARENTLY DIED an unhappy man. His final
opportunity to influence the immediate future of
Israel was thwarted by the king's failure to do what
Elisha hoped he would do. But the king did not know
what Elisha wanted. Elisha wanted him to beat the floor
five or six times (instead of three). But I don't think the
king did anything wrong.

Let's look at the passage here:

Now when Elisha had fallen sick with the illness
of which he was to die, Joash king of Israel went

down to him and wept before him, crying, "My
father, my father! The chariots of Israel and its
horsemen!" And Elisha said to him, "Take a bow
and arrows." So he took a bow and arrows. Then
he said to the king of Israel, "Draw the bow," and
he drew it. And Elisha laid his hands on the king's
hands. And he said, "Open the window eastward,"
and he opened it. Then Elisha said, "Shoot," and
he shot. And he said, "The LORD's arrow of victory,
the arrow of victory over Syria! For you shall fight
the Syrians in Aphek until you have made an end of
them." And he said, "Take the arrows," and he took
them. And he said to the king of Israel, "Strike the
ground with them." And he struck three times and
stopped. Then the man of God was angry with him
and said, "You should have struck five or six times;
then you would have struck down Syria until you
made an end of it, but now you will strike down
Syria only three times." So Elisha died, and they
buried him. Now bands of Moabites used to invade
the land in the spring of the year. And as a man was
being buried, behold, a marauding band was seen
and the man was thrown into the grave of Elisha,
and as soon as the man touched the bones of Elisha,
he revived and stood on his feet.

—2 KINGS 13:14–21

Yes, Elisha had double the anointing of Elijah. He
asked for it and got it. I have thought of making a study
of whether Elisha's anointing could have been double in
quality rather than quantity. Some of Elisha's miracles are
so beyond imagining that I have thought maybe Elisha
did have double Elijah's anointing in quality. But probably

not. By the accounts in 1 Kings and 2 Kings, Elisha accomplished *double the number* of Elijah's miracles—the last being after Elisha died.

I would therefore reckon the double anointing Elisha had in terms of quantity. We know that Elisha was an ambitious man; only an ambitious person would have the audacity to ask for double the anointing of Elijah.

However, Elijah and Elisha were different. Elisha did not have Elijah's charisma—his rather flamboyant personality. Elisha did not boast of being the "only" prophet left. Elijah's self-pity—"I am no better than my forefathers," wondering about his place in history (1 Kings 19:4)—was not mirrored in Elisha. As for the one hundred prophets, they were around in Elijah's time but hung around Elisha after Elijah was transported. Elisha was willing to be "one of the boys." He did not show fearfulness as Elijah did when Jezebel vowed to come after him. Elijah was just like us, as James 5:17 says.

The last several passages regarding Elisha show three things: (1) he was beginning to slow down, (2) he did not have a spectacular end, (3) nor did he have a successor. Perhaps he thought one of the hundred sons of prophets would do this. To think very much on this would be, I believe, unprofitable speculation.

Elisha was a truly great man. I think his refusal to meet Naaman at first showed this. He did not try to impress the Syrian general. As I said too, Elisha's not making sure that Naaman found out about Gehazi's lie showed his greatness. Elisha knew that God knew the truth, and that was enough for him. This is to say nothing about the other miracles. But he died a disappointed man. We cannot be sure what he hoped to accomplish that he did not accomplish.

The transparent truth is that they were both ordinary men. It was the Spirit of God on them that made them great. As I said, James wants all people to know that Elijah—the one who would be remembered in history far more than Elisha—was an ordinary man!

Although Elisha had twice the miracles, Elijah was the prophet people would remember. The Old Testament closes with a reference to Elijah (Mal. 4:5–6). It is Elijah whom the angel Gabriel mentions when he appears to Zechariah (Luke 1:17). It is Elijah who appears with Moses on the Mount of Transfiguration (Matt. 17:3). At the cross the people said of Jesus, "He's calling for Elijah" (Mark 15:35).

Elisha was pretty much forgotten after he died.

Elisha did not have the spectacular homegoing that Elijah had, but God affirmed Elisha in a way that is beautiful. A nameless dead man who was thrown into Elisha's grave suddenly came to life! It is a manifest way of God showing His pleasure with Elisha. Elisha may have been disappointed, but God was pleased; that is what matters.

What is going on here with regard to Elisha's bones bringing a man to life? Elisha's miracle after his death is the basis some use to pray to the saints. This is the basis some use for the idea of "grave sucking," a bizarre way of trying to get a dead person's anointing. Those who do this get nothing good and possibly something bad; I would be more fearful of getting a demon when carrying on such an unbiblical practice.

Once again: Elisha may have died in disappointment; he did not accomplish all he wanted. Yet he received his "well done" from God the moment he died. Elisha's spirit was not in the grave; he was given a spiritual body. God gave His opinion for all to see: this was a man who pleased God.

If you read this book with the hope of getting a double anointing, I understand that. I would like that too. This anointing comes to the undeserving, ordinary people who are willing to put the honor of God above the praise of man (John 5:44). I know some who are worried about men's applause and opinion after they are gone. The truth is, that will not matter at all! It is better to get God's applause and opinion of us after we are gone.

By the way, note how 2 Kings 13 ends: "Three times Joash defeated [the king of Syria] and recovered the cities of Israel" (v. 25). Just as Elisha predicted.

Elisha may not have been transported to Heaven as Elijah was. But I would welcome receiving the praise of God as Elisha did. That's a pretty good ending, if you ask me.

NOTES

INTRODUCTION

1. William Carey, BrainyQuote, accessed November 8, 2021, https://www.brainyquote.com/quotes/william_carey_404660.
2. Joel Killion, "Respectability VS the Anointing—Paul Cain (May 1991)," *Fair Haven* (blog), May 18, 2015, https://joelkillion.com/2015/05/18/respectability-vs-the-anointing-paul-cain-may-1991/.

CHAPTER 1

1. Bible Tools, s.v. *"chrio,"* accessed November 8, 2021, https://www.bibletools.org/index.cfm/fuseaction/Lexicon.show/ID/G5548/chrio.htm.

CHAPTER 2

1. Bible Study Tools, s.v. *"telos,"* accessed November 9, 2021, https://www.biblestudytools.com/lexicons/greek/nas/telos.html.
2. Martyn Lloyd-Jones, AZ Quotes, accessed November 9, 2021, https://www.azquotes.com/quote/1412159.

CHAPTER 3

1. Amelia Hull, "Life for a Look," Hymnary.org, accessed November 12, 2021, "https://hymnary.org/text/there_is_life_for_a_look_at_the_crucifie.

2. J. Hart, "Come Ye Sinners, Poor and Needy,"
Hymnary.org, 1759, https://hymnary.org/text/come_
ye_sinners_poor_and_needy_weak_and.

CHAPTER 4

1. Martin Luther, AZ Quotes, accessed November
16. 2021, https://www.azquotes.com/author/9142-
Martin_Luther/tag/music.

CHAPTER 6

1. Tony Hart, "Being Grateful Is Healthy," Mayo
Clinic Connect, November 9, 2016, https://
connect.mayoclinic.org/blog/mayo-clinic-advocates/
newsfeed-post/being-grateful-is-healthy/.

CHAPTER 16

1. Lexico, s.v. "siege," accessed February 1, 2022,
https://www.lexico.com/definition/siege.